Air New Zealand: Celebrating 75 Years

Published by Bauer Media Group (NZ) LP
Shed 12, City Works Depot
90 Wellesley Street
Auckland 1010
New Zealand
www.bauermedia.co.nz

© 2014

ISBN 9780473302511

Air New Zealand Project Manager
Andrea Dale
Archive Research Andrea Hemmins
Editor Jenny Farrell
Design inhousedesign.co.nz
Text Paul Little
Picture Research Becky Masters

Printed in New Zealand by McCollams
www.mccollams.co.nz

Contents

Sky pioneers 6

1940 —1949 8
TEAL deal 14
The first flight 18
Waiting in the wings 22
Crest of a wave 24
Local heroes 32
The war effort 34
Poster office 36
High-flying dining 38

1950 —1959 40
Coral harmony 48
Pacific promises 54
Regal pedigree 56
Official opening of 60
Wellington Airport
Ed in the clouds 62
Women in uniforms 64
Child's play 66

1960—1969 68
Beatlemania hits 76
New Zealand
Freight expectations 78
TEAL turns 21 in style 80
Stamps of approval 81
High exposure 82
An air of sophistication 84
LA times 86
It's all in the name 88
The way they wore 90
The jet set 94
International arrival 98
Tag team 100

1970—1979 102
The final touchdown 110
The pilots' plane 112
The computer revolution 114
National treasures 116
Two become one 122
Anything for a laugh 124
Sea and sky 125
Plane clothes operatives 126
Flight TE901 128

1980—1989 132
Enter the jumbo 140
Soaring high above the 142
heavens
A change in the air 144
London calling 146
Home comforts 150
Drama at Nadi 152
The scenic route 153
Pride and joy 154
Koru Care begins 155
Private life 156

1990—1999 158
50th Anniversary 166
Pacific Wave campaign 167
At your service 168
Suits staff down to 172
the ground
Where there was smoke 174
Brand new day 176
The Ansett tail 178

2000—2009 182
Reversal of fortune 190
Switching gear 194
Fun and games 196
In the seat pocket 198
in front of you
Coming back down 200
to earth
What a joke 202

2010—2015 204
Trooping of the colour 212
Safe hands 214
Chair leaders 218
Greener skies 220
Brought to you by 224
Welcome to 230
Middle-earth
Black to the future 232

From the flight deck 234
Air New Zealand Fleet 236
Illustrations 238
Acknowledgements 242

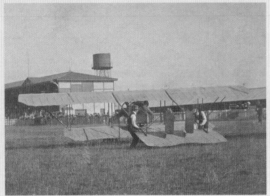

Top row, from left Orville and Wilbur Wright launch a glider in 1902; Lieutenant Joseph Hammond takes to the air over Auckland in 1914; Professor Tom Baldwin; Gordon Coates, Minister of Defence, being kitted out to fly with legendary pilot George Bolt.

Middle row, from left George Bolt; James William Humphrys "Will" Scotland's Caudron biplane; Vivian Walsh; the Walsh brothers launch a plane.

Bottom row, from left Canterbury Aviation Company; Sir Charles Kingsford Smith's *Southern Cross*; Sir Charles Kingsford Smith; Bert Mercer of Air Travel (NZ) Ltd.

Sky pioneers

Before there was NAC or TEAL, there were enterprising aviation enthusiasts who fostered a proud tradition of flying in New Zealand. Without their determination, we might not be where we are today.

The importance of air travel to New Zealand – given its remote and hard-to-access regions – cannot be overstated and it didn't take long to get started in this country. Debate still rages about whether Cantabrian Richard Pearse managed sustained controlled flight before Orville and Wilbur Wright's successful effort in 1903 – but his passion for innovation inaugurated a great airborne tradition.

The first manned flight in New Zealand actually took place in January 1889 – just not in a plane: American balloonist Professor Baldwin conducted a display for a crowd in Dunedin.

In 1913, according to the Air Force Museum of New Zealand, Second Lieutenant Joseph Hammond became the country's first Government pilot, giving demonstrations at Auckland's Epsom Showgrounds in 1914. He flew in *Britannia*, a Blériot XI-2 that was a gift from Britain.

Meanwhile, in February 1914, James William Humphrys "Will" Scotland flew from Invercargill to Gore, making the first cross-country flight, before carrying on to Dunedin, Timaru, Christchurch and Wellington, where he crashed. He also carried some of the first airmail, dropping a letter in Christchurch and a parcel to a friend in Temuka as he flew over. "There was nothing breakable in it," he noted.

A year later in Auckland, brothers Leo and Vivian Walsh founded the New Zealand Flying School at Kohimarama and a year after that, in 1915, Henry Wigram founded the Canterbury Aviation Company. Between them, the two enterprises trained nearly 300 pilots – many of whom went to fly in World War I: despite the tragic loss of young life, they were certain the war would improve technology and create demand for commercial air transport.

The Right Rev HW Cleary, Catholic Bishop of Auckland, is credited with being the country's first genuine fare-paying passenger: in 1919 he used a New Zealand Flying School seaplane to visit parishioners in Coromandel.

In 1920, Rudolph Wigley founded the New Zealand Aero Transport Company in Timaru and in 1928, Australian aviator Sir Charles Kingsford Smith made the first trans-Tasman flight – he was an adventurer at heart but one of his primary motives was the hope of winning a government mail contract.

But it would be 15 years before commercial aviation really took off – the first regular scheduled air service was by Bert Mercer's Hokitika-based Air Travel (NZ) Ltd, which flew the West Coast in a de Havilland Fox Moth in 1934. By the end of the decade, every major town had an air service.

And no description of pioneering flyers would be complete without Jean Batten, who in 1936 flew solo from England to New Zealand – 14,224 miles in 11 days and 45 minutes. A stunning effort, and a worthy tradition.

Above Jean Batten made history when she completed the first solo flight from England to New Zealand.

(10) **History: 1940-1949**
Milestones and other memorable moments from the decade.

(14) **TEAL deal**
How a variety of motives led to the formation of the national carrier.

(18) **The first flight**
A close-up look at TEAL's debut.

(22) **Waiting in the wings**
Stewardesses get the go-ahead to board.

(24) **Crest of a wave**
Flying boats were the first airborne experience for many.

(32) **Local heroes**
The other national airline takes to the sky.

(34) **The war effort**
World War II had a major influence on the development of Air New Zealand.

(36) **Poster office**
Early graphics recall the romance of early flight.

(38) **High-flying dining**
First-rate meals are a vital part of travellers' experience.

=1949

In August 1939, Tasman Empire Airways Limited (TEAL) – later to become Air New Zealand – was incorporated and went into business with three Short S30 Empire-class flying boats ordered from Britain, although only two would make it here.

The enterprise built on an already proud tradition of New Zealand aviation endeavour, with names such as Richard Pearse, the Walsh Brothers and Jean Batten already having made their mark.

Inevitably, the decade was dominated by World War II, with many fine flyers who would go on to careers with the local airline distinguishing themselves in combat.

The first TEAL flight – and also the first trans-Tasman airmail delivery – took place on 30 April 1940 when ZK-AMA *Aotearoa*, a Short S30 flying boat, made the journey to Sydney from Auckland in a time of nine hours.

Elsewhere, in Australia and beyond, travellers could take connecting flights east to the United States, and west to the United Kingdom. Thus ended the tyranny of distance for New Zealanders, who would soon gain a reputation as the world's greatest travellers, thanks in no small part to their national airline.

By decade's end, TEAL had opened a sales office at Mechanics Bay in Auckland, and was flying up to seven return trips a week between New Zealand and Australia.

The National Airways Corporation, better known as NAC, began flying on 1 April 1947. It would later become exclusively a domestic airline performing the vital function of connecting New Zealand's towns and cities – locations as remote as Whangarei, Hokitika and Invercargill were among its first destinations. But in its early days NAC also flew the Pacific, to Norfolk Island, Fiji, Tonga, Samoa and the Cook Islands.

Both airlines expanded their operations during the rest of the decade. Freight and mail were an important part of their business at the start and would remain so.

In 1949, TEAL's Solent flying-boat flagship, ZK-AML *Aotearoa II* was christened by Princess Elizabeth in Belfast. On its delivery flight it set a record of five hours and 37 minutes for crossing the Tasman.

Thus ended the tyranny of distance for New Zealanders, who would soon gain a reputation as the world's greatest travellers, thanks in no small part to their national airline.

Top TEAL's base in 1948, at Mechanics Bay in downtown Auckland, home to the flying boats.

Above TEAL signage on the Mechanics Bay sales office, 1946.

Above right Speedy delivery of mail was a priority for the airline from its inception.

Top right Princess Elizabeth launches the flagship flying boat *Aotearoa II* in Belfast.

Right Reels documenting the 1948 Olympics are unloaded – before television, sports fans had to rely on film for their coverage.

August 1939

In August 1939, the incorporation of Tasman Empire Airways Limited (TEAL) was sufficiently advanced for ZK-AMA *Aotearoa* to fly to New Zealand.

30 April 1940

The inaugural weekly Auckland-Sydney flight of the *Aotearoa*, commanded by Captain John Burgess and carrying nine passengers.

August 1940

TEAL increases the frequency of its Auckland-Sydney service to three flights a fortnight.

31 March 1941

TEAL's first annual report shows a profit of $2,724,389 in today's dollars.

Top right Portrait of Tasman Empire Airways Captain John Burgess, who flew the first Auckland-Sydney flight.

Right An early example of air-to-air photography shows the *Aotearoa* flying over Auckland.

1942

During the year to 31 March, TEAL flies several charter and reconnaissance flights to New Caledonia, Fiji, Tonga, Samoa and Hawaii to assist the war effort.

June 1944

The 1000th crossing of the Tasman.

17 July 1946

TEAL takes delivery of the first of its Tasman-class flying boats, ZK-AMB *Tasman*, which arrives from the UK.

HISTORICAL EVENTS IN NEW ZEALAND
1940—49

1940

- 5 January: First Echelon of the 2nd New Zealand Expeditionary Force leaves for the Middle East (left).
- 20 August: German raider *Orion* sinks the steamer *Turakina* off Cape Egmont.

- Conscription for military service.
- Germans lay mines across Hauraki Gulf.
- Jockey Y-fronts go on sale (right).

December 1946

By summer, TEAL is operating seven return flights a week across the Tasman.

1 April 1947

New Zealand National Airways Corporation (NAC) begins licensed operations, serving Kaitaia, Kaikohe, Whangarei, Auckland, Tauranga, Gisborne, Napier, New Plymouth, Palmerston North, Wellington, Blenheim, Nelson, Christchurch, Dunedin, Invercargill, Westport, Greymouth and Hokitika.

TASMAN EMPIRE AIRWAYS LTD.

1947

NAC also begins Pacific services to Norfolk Island, Fiji, Tonga, Samoa and the Cook Islands.

26 May 1949

TEAL's Solent flying-boat flagship, ZK-AML *Aotearoa II* is christened by Princess Elizabeth in Belfast.

14 November 1949

Solent ZK-AMM *Ararangi* begins Auckland-Sydney service.

7 December 1949

On its delivery flight, *Aotearoa II* crosses the Tasman in a record five hours 37 minutes.

Top left TEAL's winged letterhead insignia.

Left Local dignitaries pose in front of Lockheed Electra *Kahu* at the opening of the NAC Northland Air Service, Kaikohe, 1947.

Top right Unloading luggage from an NAC Dominic aircraft at Rongotai.

Right The NAC mail plane *Kahu* attracts a crowd at the opening of the Northland Air Service at Onerahi Airport, Whangarei.

1941
- New Zealand forces suffer heavy losses in the Battle of Crete.
- First US troops arrive in New Zealand.

- New Zealand declares war on Japan following the attack on Pearl Harbor (left).
- Mobilisation of women for essential work.
- Death penalty abolished.

1942
- Women become eligible to sit on juries.

1947
- Mabel Howard becomes first woman Cabinet minister (right).
- Expatriate artist Frances Hodgkins dies (far right).
- Assisted Immigration Scheme – suspended during World War II – resumes.

1949
- New Zealanders become "British subjects and New Zealand citizens".
- Referendum votes for compulsory military training.

TEAL deal

The history of Air New Zealand begins with the formation of Tasman Empire Airways Ltd (TEAL), a move driven by a combination of political and commercial interests.

An airline to serve New Zealand had naturally been the subject of discussion for many years before it came into being: a plan for a New Zealand-based company to fly between New Zealand and Australia had been drafted in 1934 by Britain's Imperial Airways Australian representative.

The Australian, British and New Zealand governments all approved the plan, but, as well as a war to hold things up, there were numerous disagreements among the three parties. "I think the words that flowed would have floated a flying boat, or sunk it," noted Qantas Empire Airways chairman Hudson Fysh.

A major factor driving the decision was the desire to link the furthest arms of the British Empire into one embrace. Before TEAL it was possible to fly from Britain to Australia – in many stages – but to continue on to New Zealand would be the last link in the imperial chain. The mail would get through and the more visionary among those involved could see the commercial possibilities dimly in the future.

New Zealand, remote from even its nearest neighbours, was unable to contemplate having an airline until it had aircraft that could fly at least as far as the 2100km to Australia without stopping. The advent of the S30 Empire class opened up this possibility. Unlike earlier planes, it did not need to refuel every 800km or so.

Originally New Zealand was a minority shareholder in its national airline. When it was registered on 26 April 1940, the shareholders were Qantas/Australia with 23 percent, BOAC/Britain with 38 percent, the Union Steamship Company/Union Airways, 19 percent and the New Zealand government, 20 percent. Nevertheless, the government was keenly interested in TEAL's profitability and the consequent tax take. (In 1953, the Australian and New Zealand governments would become joint equal and sole shareholders in the company.)

The Union Steamship Company, in the form of Union Airways, had ordered three of the Short Brothers Empire-class S30 flying boats from the British government.

The *Aotearoa* arrived first but with the advent

TEAL staff in front of
the flying boat Awatere
at Mechanics Bay,
Auckland, 1950.

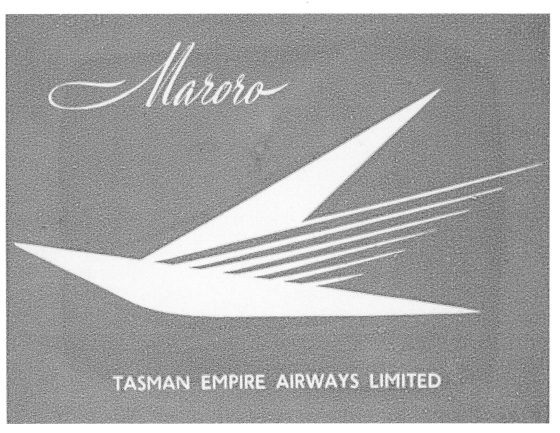

Maroro

TASMAN EMPIRE AIRWAYS LIMITED

of war the *Australia* was lost to the airline. It had been damaged and before it could be repaired and delivered, it was deemed necessary for the war effort. A service could not be run with only one plane and it was only when the *Awarua* arrived that regular services between Auckland and Sydney commenced.

The war, which had suppressed so much normal economic activity, also held back the development of TEAL's business. In its first year of operations after the war, the airline carried three times as many passengers, three times as much freight and 50 percent more mail than it had in the 1941-42 year.

The most memorable flight of the decade was almost certainly that of the *New Zealand* on 3 December 1947, which led to TEAL's fleet of Sandringhams, the aircraft which had joined the fleet in 1946, being grounded for six months. Carrying 29 passengers and six crew from Sydney to Auckland, the *New Zealand* suffered an engine failure, and it was decided to turn back. It continued to lose altitude until it was flying just 15m above the sea.

According to one account, Captain Patterson ordered all 1587kg of freight, mail and baggage dumped. "This had to be done carefully from the front and rear hatches simultaneously in order not to upset the aircraft's equilibrium," Neil Rennie wrote in *Conquering Isolation*.

"What caused the greatest fuss later was the loss of the ecclesiastical vestments of Episcopalian Bishop Ashton Oldham, as he lodged an astonishingly large insurance claim for them.

"More noteworthy was First Officer Frank Kilgour's feat in singlehandedly dumping a 600lb [272kg] plastic die which had taken four men to load. The reduced load had the desired effect."

It was an encouraging beginning for the airline, however. The decade began with 130 single trans-Tasman trips carrying a total of 1461 passengers in its first year. In 1949, it made 876 trips carrying a total of 24,522 passengers.

The first flight

Those on board the first flight of the fledgling TEAL were present for what was a momentous occasion by any standards, marking an important stage in New Zealand's development as a nation.

Captain John Burgess checked the fuel cocks were turned on, the airscrews in fully fine pitch, the wing flaps a quarter out, and all instruments were reading normal. He glanced at his watch, nodded to First Officer W.J. Craig and with practised skill firmly thrust forward the four throttles on the quadrant to the take-off power position.

Outside and behind him the noise from the four Bristol Perseus engines surged to a reassuring crescendo as at maximum rpm and 30 inches of boost, they delivered their combined output of 3650hp. The Short S30 Empire flying boat *Aotearoa* ceased drifting gently on the tide, shuddered as the thrust from four propellers began urging her forward, and slowly gathered way down the Waitemata Harbour. Inside her spacious hull, the nine passengers watched waves and spray rise up and engulf the forward cabin windows, the sound of water hammering on the hull mingling with the roar from the engines. *Aotearoa* accelerated to 65mph and the water noise diminished as the hull climbed up on the step. After a minute or so, speed reached 110mph and Captain Burgess lifted the

30 tons of aircraft smoothly into the air. He made a gentle climbing turn onto a compass bearing of almost due west, the course for Sydney, and at a sedate 200ft a minute ascended with the dawn to the cruising altitude of 5000ft.

The date was 30 April 1940. TEAL's first scheduled flight was launched.

Officialdom marked the event with a state dinner in Auckland and a modest ceremony in the pre-dawn darkness before take-off attended by about 50 people; New Zealand's Minister of Aviation (and, just as significantly, postmaster-general) the Hon. F. Jones, spoke, the chairman of TEAL and Union Airways, Colonel Norrie Falla, responded, Jones cut a white ribbon across the Braby pontoon, and the passengers and crew boarded.

For Captain John Burgess and his crew, the simple pre-flight preparations had begun the night before with a phone call to the meteorological office to check the weather across the Tasman. The Auckland-Sydney flight was against the prevailing westerlies and the estimated strength of the headwinds dictated

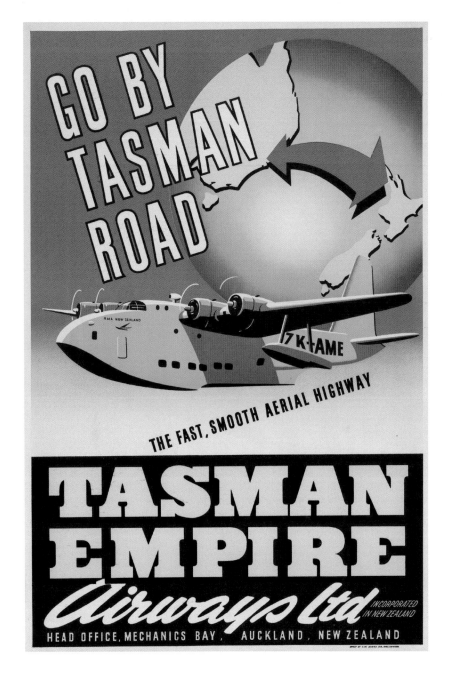

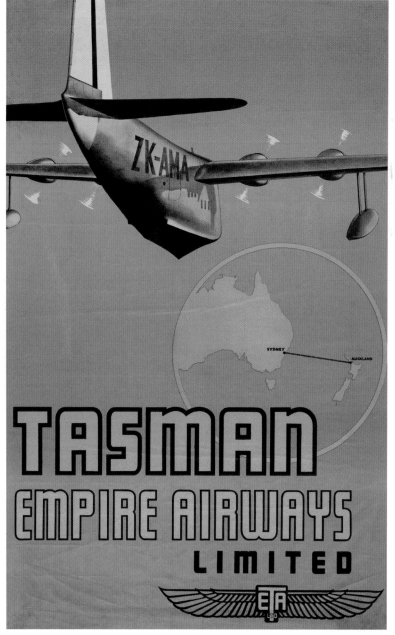

Far left Early passengers were encouraged to think of their journey as a road in the sky.

Left Australia was and still is a popular destination for New Zealanders.

Top Flight crew and passengers on the *Aotearoa*'s pontoon at Mechanics Bay.

Above Spectators watch as the *Aotearoa* leaves its pontoon.

the combined weight of passengers and mail carried and the fuel load; Second Officer C.A. Macdonald checked the engines and aircraft systems. Chief Steward R.A. Phillips supervised the stowage of the mail bags containing 41,000 letters, then in the early morning loaded the passengers' luggage.

Although it was the first scheduled flight, for Burgess and his crew it was all very much routine. Burgess had flown the first Empire flying boat, *Centaurus*, out from England to New Zealand in 1937 on an initial tour-proving flight. He had also flown *Aotearoa* on its delivery flight to New Zealand in August 1939, and this same crew now on board had carried out tour-proving fights across the Tasman, to Fiji, Tonga and Western Samoa, and to different harbours in New Zealand.

While *Aotearoa* was still passing over Auckland, one passenger, Hudson Fysh, leaned over to another, A.E. Rudder, and cheerfully paid him five shillings in settlement of a bet that the service would not start that day. Fysh, chairman of Qantas Empire Airways, and Rudder, Australasian representative of Imperial Airways, were both directors of TEAL. Also on board were G.C. Whyte, one of the two New Zealand representatives on the TEAL board and E.C. Johnston, Assistant Director-General of Civil Aviation in Australia. The passenger list also included Harvey (later Sir Harvey) Turner of Auckland, later a director of TEAL for seven years, who had booked his £30 one-way ticket three years earlier, and two women whose daring the Auckland newspapers commented on with some astonishment. They were Miss Joan Hewitt, a New Zealand author and journalist, and Miss Patty Dromgool (later Mrs B.P. Whelan) making a trip to Sydney instead of a long-planned trip to England cancelled because of the war. The other two passengers were T.C. Webster and H.O. Browne.

As *Aotearoa* settled at a cruising altitude of 5000ft and a speed of 147mph, First Officer Craig, whose prime responsibility was navigation, busied himself with the task of determining the aircraft's track and groundspeed. To do this Captain Burgess altered the heading 30 degrees to port then 30 degrees to starboard off course while Craig squinted down through the drift sight at the sea's surface, and noted how many degrees of drift the aircraft was making in relation to each compass heading.

With the aid of a course and distance calculator, known as a CDC, he established the actual strength and direction of the wind and the aircraft's groundspeed. It differed slightly from the forecast wind, so after some quick calculations on his navigational slide rule and replotting on the Mercator Chart, he gave John Burgess a new heading. Captain Burgess set this in the autopilot.

The autopilot eliminated the strain of having to fly the aeroplane every minute of the way, but could not be left unmonitored for very long as it drifted off heading. Craig unpacked his sextant and stepped into the astrodome where he "shot" the sun, now 20 degrees above the horizon. He called the altitudes out to radio operator F.L. Williams who wrote them down and noted the times taken from the chronometer. Craig then averaged the six single shot readings and calculated and plotted a position line. These single sunlines were an important check on the aircraft's position throughout the journey and would be made at about hourly intervals.

Along with bearings from radio stations picked up on the radio direction finder (RDF) these sunlines, in conjunction with dead reckoning calculations of groundspeed and windspeed from the drift sight, were the only means of navigation. The primitive RDF was only accurate when within about 1000 miles of the station, depending on the station's signal power. Craig handed the radio operator a message slip which gave the aircraft's position in degrees and minutes of latitude and longitude, and a weather summary, which Williams transmitted back to Auckland in code on his Morse key. This would be the routine for the rest of the nine-hour journey. Unlike so many subsequent Tasman crossings, the weather remained calm and there was little turbulence to disturb the smoothness of *Aotearoa*'s passage. The passengers were able to enjoy a magnificent breakfast served hot from large vacuum jars loaded just before take-off, and later an equally superb lunch.

Towards 3pm, the coast of Australia appeared on the horizon. The pointer on the dial of the RDF, tuned into a Sydney radio station, indicated they were on track for Rose Bay, the flying-boat base. Some anxious searching by binoculars soon confirmed the correct landmarks were in view. At precisely 3.30pm New Zealand time, after nine hours' flying, John Burgess set *Aotearoa* smoothly down on the harbour near the launch from which the control officer had earlier cleared the landing area of any stray launches and boats before signaling it was safe to land. Burgess expertly taxied the flying boat up to its mooring. The rope was tied around the bollard in the bow and the engines were cut and TEAL's first flight was over. Passengers and crew disembarked aboard the control officer's launch and the first of many thousands of TEAL passengers were carried safely to the shore.

Reprinted with permission from Conquering Isolation *by Neil Rennie, Heinemann Reed, 1990*

Waiting in the wings

There was reluctance to employ women on the flying boats initially but in 1946 the first six stewardesses joined TEAL, becoming the face of the airline for many. Passengers' safety was always a large part of their duties, and in the early years they had to be unmarried.

Left TEAL's first six stewardesses began on the flying boats in 1946.

Right Stewardesses with children for a publicity photograph at Mechanics Bay. *Sandringham* flying boat in background.

Crest of a wave

The flying boats that were standard in the earliest years of commercial flight helped develop and popularise the concept of air travel for many.

Behind the homely designation Short S25 Sunderland Mark III lies one of the most beautiful forms of transport ever invented. Flying boats were early leaders in air transport because of their versatility.

They had one supreme advantage over other types of aircraft – they didn't need a runway, let alone an airport. They could land on the water and taxi to a wharf or unload passengers onto a boat that would take them to land. This meant their potential destinations were, theoretically, only limited to anywhere near water.

This made possible a number of tourism developments that would change the face of travel. A Pacific island-hopping Coral Route on which the aircraft landed on a coal-black tarmac rather than azure waters wouldn't have been the same.

Following TEAL's first purchases of Short

Solents and two Catalinas borrowed from the air force, the airline bought four Mark IV Solents.

The last of the flying boats to be designed by the Short brothers, the Mark IV was the pinnacle of that model's incarnations, at least in part because TEAL had them produced to its specifications. They could accommodate 45 passengers on two decks linked by a spiral staircase. The fittings set a new standard in comfort with winged headrests and the essential antimacassar to prevent the greasy hair creams of the day marring the upholstery. Everyone had a reading light and air vent.

A key shift demonstrated by the inclusion of these creature comforts was that from a view of air travel as a sometimes necessary evil, to something to be done for enjoyment and its own

sake. But as airports became established around the country, the flying boats lost their *raison d'être* and their days were numbered. Pragmatism would triumph over paradise.

The beginning of the end came in 1954 when DC-6 aircraft began flying the trans-Tasman route from Whenuapai. The conversion was complete by 1960.

The flying boats lasted longer than they might have thanks largely to political motives. Many aspects of the company's – and domestic airline NAC's – workings had their basis in a government desire to show loyalty to Britain, which was often at odds with commercial sense.

As glamorous as the Mark IV Solents were, the decision to buy them in 1949 was not

popular with those who could see that the future of air travel lay with land-based flying in aircraft which had the potential to carry even greater numbers of passengers as they developed. But the Solents were British and DC-4s, which would have been the more commercially sensible choice, were American.

After this purchase TEAL was out of the flying-boat business for good, although the last aircraft continued to fly the Coral Route until 1960.

Neither of TEAL's original two aircraft has survived, but the last of the Solents, ZK-AMO *Aranui*, can be seen at Auckland's Museum of Transport and Technology, allowing 21st century enthusiasts to experience just a little of the magic of this extraordinary means of flight.

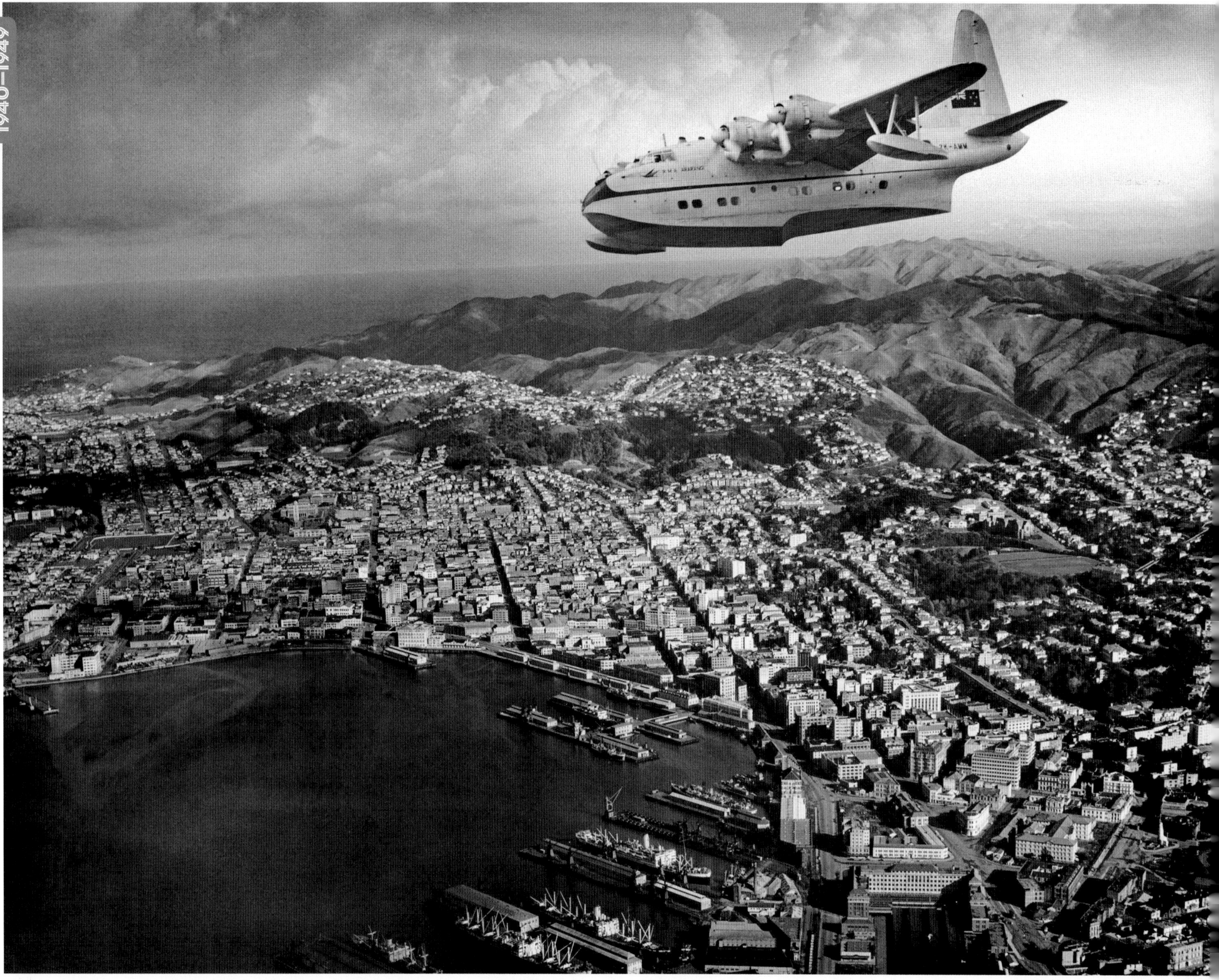

Left A Solent makes a spectacular pass over Wellington.

Above A Solent landing at Evans Bay, Wellington, photographed from Mt Victoria.

Top right Plenty of room for the whole family.

Right Service with a smile on board TEAL Solent flying boat Ararangi.

Far left Heading to Australia for a rugby tour in 1951, members of the All Blacks are transported by launch to ZK-AML *Aotearoa II*.

Below far left A TEAL employee mooring the *Awarua* at Mechanics Bay.

Left The sight of the flying boats taking off never failed to captivate children.

Below left Marie Vallin boarding at Mechanics Bay, 6 September 1949.

This page ZK-AMA *Aotearoa* makes the 1000th crossing of the Tasman, at Mechanics Bay, June 1944.

Local heroes

No less essential than an airline to connect New Zealand with the rest of the world was an airline that would help New Zealanders stay connected with each other – hence the birth of the National Airways Corporation.

The National Airways Corporation (NAC) was formed in 1947 under Peter Fraser's Labour government, which wanted a state-owned, public-service domestic airline.

As James S. Martin explains in his unpublished history *The Way It Used to Be*, NAC was formed by firstly, "civilianisation of 40 squadron. Surplus to air force requirements, their fleet of 20-plus passenger DC-3 aircraft, aircrew and their expertise were a ready 'off the shelf' airline in waiting. [Secondly,] nationalisation of the privately run domestic airlines including: Air Travel (NZ) Ltd, Cook Strait Airways, East Coast Airways and Union Airways, the Union Steamship Company subsidiary and the largest of the four."

All this was a result of a 1945 study by Air Vice Marshal Sir Arthur Neville – as Vice Chief of Air Staff he had authored *The Way Ahead*, a document that became the post-war blueprint for civil aviation.

Left An early NAC poster.

Far Right Friendly service to all age groups was always a hallmark of the NAC style and an obvious selling point in promotional material.

Far below right Passengers and crew on NAC's inaugural flight recieved certificates to mark the occasion.

Its fleet consisted of a mixed assortment of aircraft, but it was the DC-3 that would become so closely associated with the airline for the best part of 20 years. Vickers Viscounts for main routes, and Fokker Friendships servicing the regions, would also be conspicuous on NAC.

NAC and TEAL thus came into the world with different commercial agendas. The international airline's job was to connect the country with the world and show a profit. The domestic airline's job was to keep the country connected for the social and economic benefits that would result, even if it meant cross-subsidies, under which unprofitable routes would be propped up by the revenue from better-patronised ones.

At the time of its establishment, NAC was serving Kaitaia, Kaikohe, Whangarei, Auckland, Tauranga, Gisborne, Napier, New Plymouth, Palmerston North, Wellington, Blenheim, Nelson, Christchurch, Dunedin, Invercargill, Westport, Greymouth and Hokitika.

Before the air route was established, the journey from Auckland to Invercargill, for instance, took three days, involving trains, boats and a lot of waiting in between.

Aviation writer Geoffrey Thomas summed up how much work there was to be done to create a fully fledged local network: "When NAC started operations, the only airports with all-weather runways were at Auckland, Paraparaumu and Woodbourne. Christchurch opened its runway in 1950 and Dunedin did not have a sealed runway until 1962.

"The lack of suitable runways was matched by the lack of suitable ground navigation aids, contributing to the loss of two aircraft in 1948 and 1949. Pilots could tune into a few radio stations to get their bearings but flying was mostly by the 'seat of the pants'.

"New Zealand airlines suffered with the lack of suitable infrastructure because airports were largely controlled by local councils. The government itself did not have the necessary vision to make the required investment decisions."

In its early days, NAC was also an international airline. It took over flying to the

Pacific Islands, including Norfolk Island, before becoming a solely domestic operation in the mid-1950s.

In 1956 NAC appointed its first air hostesses, flying on DC-3s on the main trunk routes. There had been a campaign to employ hostesses for some time but management had resisted because of the expense. The tipping point was the 1954 crash at Paraparaumu where everyone was saved except two children who many thought might have survived had hostesses with their safety training been on hand to assist.

With entry into the jet age unavoidable, NAC resisted strong political pressure to buy British, and opted to upgrade its fleet to Boeing 737s. The government was not pleased to be thus embarrassed, especially at a time of concern over continued access to European markets for New Zealand trade.

Furthermore, the Boeing aircraft were still in the planning stage, while the British option was already available. History, however, proved the carrier's management to have made the correct choice: the bigger and cheaper 737 was an excellent, reliable aeroplane.

Nevertheless, NAC struggled financially with the dual burden of profit expectations and a commitment to maintain unprofitable routes. (When a merger with Air New Zealand finally took place, the older airline regarded the cross-subsidisation practice with great suspicion.)

Eventually the government decided to put its money where its social agenda had been, and told NAC to concentrate on maximising its returns. The logical and most effective way to do that was to drop some unprofitable routes and reduce frequencies on others, but as many of these involved marginal electorates, the government put the changes on hold.

Eventually, economic imperatives meant that a merger of the two national airlines was the only sensible option and in 1978 they became one company, although not without considerable complications. During its 31 years of life, however, NAC had established itself in the hearts of New Zealanders with its quintessentially Kiwi style and has left an indelible legacy.

AT YOUR SERVICE

NAC

NEW ZEALAND NATIONAL AIRWAYS CORPORATION

This is to certify that

Flight Steward R.S. Purdie
cabin member
was a passenger aboard the R.M.A. "TAKITIMU" during her inaugural flight as an airliner

Auckland April 4 1949

NEW ZEALAND NATIONAL AIRWAYS CORPORATION

The war effort

World War II saw many New Zealanders enlist to serve in the skies. After the conflict was concluded, many stayed on in the Royal New Zealand Air Force, but others would lend their battle-won skills and talents to civil aviation, becoming TEAL pilots.

Much of World War II was fought out in the air and the struggle for dominance in the skies spurred such developments as radar and improved aircraft.

It also produced thousands of skilful flyers who were keen to continue piloting civilian aircraft after 1945. But as one account points out, "The advent of war almost aborted the launch of TEAL, with the British Government trying to stop delivery of… two S30s. Only intense pressure from Deputy Prime Minister Peter Fraser saved the day and the attempt to 'cut off' New Zealand had a profound effect on the development of New Zealand aviation after the war."

The involvement of the company's aircraft in wartime missions was largely due to the fact that in 1940 the Royal New Zealand Air Force had no long-range military aircraft. TEAL's flying boats *Aotearoa* and *Awarua* were therefore pressed into service, carrying 500lb bombs and air force personnel on long-range missions in the early days of the war. Their tasks included searching for vessels sunk or damaged by mines, and several missions hunting for German raiders that had been active in the Pacific, inflicting damage on Allied vessels.

Between 1941 and 1942, TEAL undertook several special charter and reconnaissance flights to Noumea, Fiji, Tonga, Samoa and as far afield as Honolulu, to assist the war effort.

Politicians and other dignitaries were regularly carried on special TEAL flights. The most notable of these was the occasion on which New Zealand's Prime Minister Walter Nash was shot at by Americans when his plane was mistaken for a Japanese aircraft while flying back to New Zealand from a meeting in Washington, DC.

As it became increasingly risky for ships to make the journey, TEAL's other crucial wartime duty was to keep up a regular trans-Tasman service which, among other things, enabled mail to reach New Zealand troops overseas.

Left Recruitment posters for service in the sky presented an image of youthful excitement.

Below left A life of adventure and daring was promised to those who joined the air force.

Right Duty bound – RNZN personnel stand to attention on *Aotearoa* in Suva, 1940.

Poster office

Few items are more evocative of their time than TEAL's early promotional graphics.

Above George Moore, who helped design the TEAL Maroro logo, at work on a poster for the airline (right).

Right The TEAL posters set out from the start to incorporate Maori art – sometimes with a touch of Australia thrown into the mix.

TASMAN *Skyway*

TEAL

TASMAN ★ EMPIRE ★ AIRWAYS ★ LIMITED

HEAD OFFICE   AUCKLAND   NEW ZEALAND   in association with   BCPA

W. HAYTHORN-THWAITE LIMITED

winter in New Zealand

so easy by Solent

TEAL

TASMAN EMPIRE AIRWAYS LIMITED

AUSTRALIA
FLY TEAL

FLY TO NEW ZEALAND

TEAL

TASMAN EMPIRE AIRWAYS LIMITED

New Zealand holiday

FLY TEAL

FIJI
FLY TEAL

High-flying dining

Eating and drinking on board has been an important part of the flying experience ever since the first person spent more than a couple of hours in the air. TEAL led the way with the provision of first-rate meals in sometimes trying conditions.

From the early days of scrambled eggs prepared on land and carried aboard in large vacuum flasks, to today's award-winning airborne cuisine prepared by some of New Zealand's most internationally respected chefs, Air New Zealand has always prided itself on providing meals that won't be dismissed cursorily as merely "airline food".

Changing tastes in food among the public have to be reflected in what's offered on board and service can make or break a meal; cabin crew have long known this. "We tried to overlay the best qualities of the average Kiwi – naturalness, warmth and approachability… the sort of service you would get at your neighbour's barbecue party on a Sunday from his sons and daughters," says Dennis Marshall, who was head of cabin services in later years.

In the first years of the trans-Tasman route and later the Coral Route, on-board dining was a notable feature.

"The food was all cooked on board from scratch by the junior steward," says former hostess Janet Beech. "We were the first airline in the world to boil water too." (It had been believed that water would not boil at high altitudes but this was disproved by the simple experiment of boiling some.)

"There was scrambled eggs and toast for breakfast, seafood cocktails made in a billy, prawn cocktails, salad-type meals. Hot meals were prepared on board as well as morning and afternoon tea with canapés. We had a dumb waiter because flying boats had two decks, but it didn't always work. There was a circular staircase. The drinks we served were miniatures."

The legendary cabin service manager of the day, Eric Mullane, had a reputation for prickliness but there was a side to him that many cabin crews only found out about later.

"We knew we got corned beef on board," says Beech, "but we didn't know that Eric's wife cooked it. And we knew we got cake from Adams Bruce, but we didn't realise that Eric picked it up from the shop in Queen St on his way to work and took it down to Mechanics Bay."

It was that devotion to the job and the passengers in the early days that set the standard that has been maintained as part of Air New Zealand tradition to this day.

TEAL SOLENT FLYING BOAT ON TRANS-TASMAN AND
SOUTH PACIFIC AIR ROUTES

TEAL Menu

LUNCHEON

CHILLED FRUIT JUICE

CRUMBED BAKED FLOUNDER,
TARTARE SAUCE

LAMB CHOPS

GREEN PEAS   GRILLED TOMATOES

SAUTE POTATOES

FRUIT SALAD   FRESH CREAM

CREAM CHEESE   TASTY CHEESE

ASSORTED BISCUITS

FRESH FRUIT IN SEASON

TEA   COFFEE

W.S. 1

Left, top The Mechanics Bay kitchen.

Centre Performing culinary miracles in confined spaces was standard.

Below Service has taken many forms over the decades. An early offering was breakfast in bed on board.

Above A TEAL Solent luncheon menu.

Right This simple menu still required a high level of skill to prepare and present in flight.

Far right When flying was still a rarity and a special occasion, it wasn't unusual to get a special Christmas Day menu.

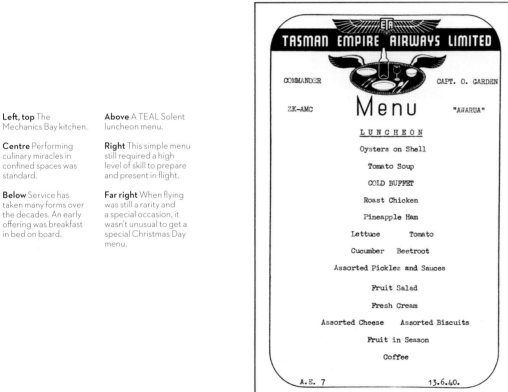

TASMAN EMPIRE AIRWAYS LIMITED

COMMANDER   CAPT. O. GARDEN

ZK–AMC   "AWARUA"

Menu

LUNCHEON

Oysters on Shell

Tomato Soup

COLD BUFFET

Roast Chicken

Pineapple Ham

Lettuce   Tomato

Cucumber   Beetroot

Assorted Pickles and Sauces

Fruit Salad

Fresh Cream

Assorted Cheese   Assorted Biscuits

Fruit in Season

Coffee

A.E. 7   13.6.40.

MENU

The Management and Staff of
Tasman Empire Airways Ltd.
wish you a Merry Christmas
and a Happy New Year

*

Christmas Day 1948

*

LUNCHEON

Cream of Tomato
Consomme Brunoise

Herrings in Tomato Sauce
Filet Mignon-Mikado
Saute Potatoes

Glazed Ham — Creamed Sweetcorn
Roast Tom Turkey — Chipolata
Salad in Season   Russian Salad

Plum Pudding — Hard and Brandy Sauces
Macedoine of Fruit in Jelly
Vanilla Ice Cream

Water Crackers
Cream Cheese   Tasty Cheese
Assorted Nuts   Fresh Fruit

Coffee

TASMAN EMPIRE AIRWAYS LIMITED

(42) History: 1950–1959
Milestones and other
memorable moments
from the decade.

(48) Coral harmony
The island-hopping route
that was to revolutionise
tourism.

(54) Pacific promises
Selling destinations with
mini-masterpieces.

(56) Regal pedigree
The Queen is one of the
world's most travelled
people, often flying with
Air New Zealand.

**(60) Official opening of
Wellington Airport**
The capital turns out to
celebrate.

(62) Ed in the clouds
TEAL was proud to bring
Hillary home.

(64) Women in uniforms
Skyborne styles are always
on the move.

(66) Child's play
Young passengers have
a special place in the
airline's heart.

=1959

The 1950s were years of consolidation and growth for TEAL and NAC, characterised by the legendary journey that became known as the Coral Route, a grand tour of Pacific islands which was pivotal to the development of local tourism and in earning TEAL a reputation for excellence in all aspects of flight.

Significant firsts were the opening of a sales office in Wellington, the country's first international cargo depot at Airways House in Auckland and the dedication of Christchurch's Harewood as an international airport.

NAC's Pacific services, except for Norfolk Island, ceased in 1952, and in 1958 it acquired its first Vickers Viscount. It also added new destinations including Whanganui and Timaru, and shed others, including Greymouth.

Flying was still seen as either an expensive luxury or an unavoidable necessity, done mainly for business, weddings and funerals – or conquering Everest, with Sir Edmund Hillary returning to New Zealand, after his triumphant ascent and subsequent tour of the United Kingdom to receive his knighthood, on a TEAL flying boat.

Another passenger who would become a regular, Queen Elizabeth II, made the first trip on a commercial airliner by a member of the British royal family when she flew from Suva to Lautoka with TEAL in 1953. The Queen also flew domestically with NAC in New Zealand.

The 1956 Melbourne Olympic Games had a big impact on airlines, requiring some innovative strategising to deal with increased passenger numbers. TEAL flew more than 4000 people to the Games.

In 1953 smaller shareholders departed, leaving the New Zealand and Australian governments joint equal owners of TEAL. In these years, the airline added three DC-6s to its fleet and several trans-Tasman destinations to its schedule, including Wellington, Christchurch, Brisbane and Melbourne. Solent flying boats – with the exception of one for the Coral Route – were phased out in this decade. In 1959 TEAL took delivery of its first jet-prop Lockheed Electra, another big step forward for the airline.

The decade was characterised by the legendary journey that became known as the Coral Route, a grand tour of Pacific islands, which earned TEAL a reputation for excellence in all aspects of flight.

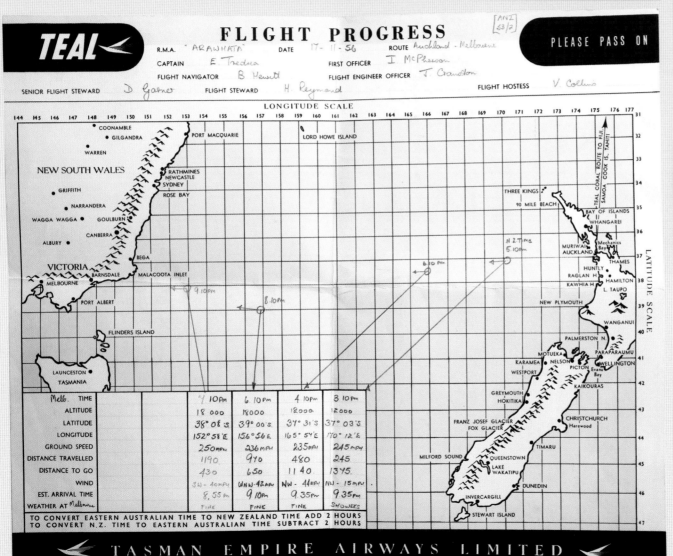

FLIGHT PROGRESS

R.M.A. "ARAWHATA"	DATE 17-11-56 ROUTE Auckland - Melbourne
CAPTAIN E. Tredrea	FIRST OFFICER I. McPherson
FLIGHT NAVIGATOR B. Hewitt	FLIGHT ENGINEER OFFICER J. Cranston
SENIOR FLIGHT STEWARD D. Garner	FLIGHT STEWARD H. Reymond FLIGHT HOSTESS V. Collins

[ANZ 53/2]

PLEASE PASS ON

LONGITUDE SCALE

Melb. TIME	7.10pm	6.10pm	4.10pm	3.10pm
ALTITUDE	18 000	18000	12000	12000
LATITUDE	38° 08'S	39° 00'S	37° 31'S	37° 03'S
LONGITUDE	152° 58'E	156° 56'E	165° 54'E	170° 12'E
GROUND SPEED	250 mph	236 mph	235 mph	245 mph
DISTANCE TRAVELLED	1190	910	480	245
DISTANCE TO GO	430	650	1140	1375
WIND	SW-40mph	WNW-42mph	NW-44mph	NW-15mph
EST. ARRIVAL TIME	8.55pm	9.10pm	9.35pm	9.35pm
WEATHER AT Melbourne	FINE	FINE	FINE	SHOWERS

TO CONVERT EASTERN AUSTRALIAN TIME TO NEW ZEALAND TIME ADD 2 HOURS
TO CONVERT N.Z. TIME TO EASTERN AUSTRALIAN TIME SUBTRACT 2 HOURS

TASMAN EMPIRE AIRWAYS LIMITED

Top left TEAL jet-prop Electra *Aotearoa*, over California, October 1959.

Top Open for business: A package is processed at the TEAL World Air Cargo office, 27 March 1951.

Above The 100th NAC Pacific flight arrives in Rarotonga, September 1951.

18 December 1950
Harewood Aerodrome, Christchurch, dedicated as an international airport.

September 1951
The 100th NAC Pacific flight.

Top and above Inside NAC's workshop at Harewood Aerodrome, 1958.

Top right Harewood seen from above. Two runways and a parallel taxiway were added this decade.

Right Loading sheep into a NAC DC-3 Freighter at Taieri Airport, Dunedin, 1957.

Far right Passengers check in at Christchurch International Airport's overseas terminal.

HISTORICAL EVENTS IN NEW ZEALAND
1950–59

1950
- Naval and ground forces sent to Korean War.
- New Zealand Legislative Council abolished.
- Wool boom, triggered by the Korean War.

- Death of Sir Apirana Ngata who contributed hugely to the revival of the Maori culture in the early 20th century (right).

27 December 1951

First Coral Route service sees TEAL flying Auckland-Papeete (Tahiti) via Suva (Fiji) and Aitutaki (Cook Islands).

June 1952

First de Havilland 114-1B Heron aircraft joins NAC fleet.

14 October 1952

Apia (Samoa) included as stopover between Suva and Aitutaki en route to Papeete.

October 1953

Reorganisation of trans-Pacific services carried out by British Commonwealth Pacific Airlines; three of its Douglas DC-6 aircraft are transferred to TEAL.

Below Crew of NAC's 100th Pacific flight pose in front of their DC-3 on arrival in Rarotonga.

Bottom Passengers board NAC's first Viscount, named "City of Wellington".

Right Local resident resting on a TEAL rowboat at Akaiami lagoon, Aitutaki, Rarotonga.

1951
- ANZUS treaty signed between United States, Australia and New Zealand.
- Maori Women's Welfare League established (right).

1952
- Population reaches more than two million.
- 23 July: Long-jump star Yvette Williams becomes first New Zealand woman to win an Olympic gold medal (left).

1953
- First tour by a reigning monarch.
- Edmund Hillary and Sherpa Tenzing Norgay, part of the British expedition, are the first to climb Mount Everest (right).

- At Opiki, Manawatu, Godfrey Bowen sets a new world record when he shears 456 full-wool ewes in nine hours.

1954
- New Zealand gains seat on United Nations Security Council.
- Mazengarb Report into juvenile delinquency released.

December 1953
Queen Elizabeth II flies with TEAL from Suva to Lautoka and return, then to Tonga in the first flights on a commercial airliner by a member of the British royal family.

January 1954
Queen Elizabeth II travels from Rotorua to Gisborne on board NAC Heron ZK-BEQ.

14 May 1954
First DC-6 Sydney-Auckland service by ZK-BGA *Aotearoa III* lands at Whenuapai Airport.

1 December 1954
Following British Commonwealth Pacific Airlines reorganisation, Australian and New Zealand governments become equal and only shareholders in TEAL.

28 October 1955
TEAL makes its 10,000th Tasman crossing.

December 1955
NAC Sunday flights commence.

Below left NAC Sunday flights commence, as advertised in the *Upper Hutt Leader*, 17 May 1956.

Below *Aotearoa III*, TEAL's first DC-6 Sydney-Auckland service by ZK-BGA, lands at Whenuapai Airport, 1954.

N.A.C. NEWS FLASH.—Sunday flights now operating main trunk and Cook Strait—yet another service to N.A.C. travellers. N.A.C. District Agents—CLARKE AGENCIES, Travel and Estate Agents, Wilkie's Arcade—office hours 8.30 a.m. to 5.30 p.m. daily, Friday nights and Saturday mornings. Tel. 3812 and 4643 (after hours.)—Advt.

1955
- Pulp and paper mill opens at Kawerau.
- The Rimutaka rail tunnel opens (right).

1956
- New Zealand troops sent to Malaya.
- Roxburgh and Whakamaru power stations in operation.

- Death of Opo the friendly dolphin in Hokianga Harbour (left).
- New Zealand's first Test cricket victory, against the West Indies at Eden Park (right).

November 1956

TEAL carries more than 4000 passengers to the Olympic Games in Melbourne. To achieve this, the company charters 10 Qantas Super Constellation flights and several DC-4s from Sabena, TAA and Qantas.

February 1957

Auckland-Melbourne service introduced as experiment and reintroduced in October as a regular operation.

January 1958

First NAC Vickers Viscount 807, ZK-BRD *City of Wellington*, arrives.

24 October 1959

Official opening of Wellington Airport.

19 November 1959

TEAL takes delivery of the first of its jet-prop Electras, ZK-TEA *Aotearoa*, flying from Burbank, California, via Nadi.

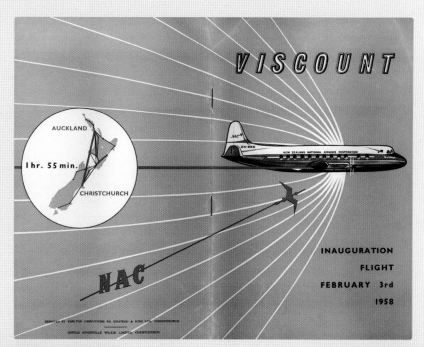

Top right An NAC booklet marks the inaugural flight of the Vickers Viscount 807 ZK-BRD.

Right Solent departing Suva's Laucala Bay pontoon, 1957.

Far right The crew of the first NAC Vickers Viscount flight is given a Maori welcome at Whenuapai Airport.

1957
- Scott Base established in Ross Dependency (right).
- Court of Appeal constituted.
- Morris Yock commences production of the Jandal.

1958
- First geothermal electricity generated at Wairakei (right).
- Auckland is first New Zealand city to introduce Barnes Dance pedestrian crossing, allowing crossing in all directions at once.

- Sir Brian Barratt-Boyes performs first open-heart surgery in New Zealand at Greenlane Hospital.

1959
- Antarctic Treaty signed with other countries involved in scientific exploration in Antarctica.
- Auckland Harbour Bridge opens (right).

- The Chinese gooseberry is renamed the kiwifruit by Turners & Growers.

The Solent flying boat
Aparima 1951-1954 arrives in
Tahiti on a "proving flight" for
TEAL's new Coral Route to a
South Seas-style welcome by
the locals.

Below, from top to bottom
Coral Route foldout fan,
menu illustration and
gummed label.

Coral harmony

Tourism was still in its infancy when the Coral Route was born, but with its promise to deliver big-city travellers from around the globe to idyllic tropical destinations in the Pacific, the service found instant popularity.

It was the epitome of romance in the skies, the ultimate pleasure flight and a one-of-a-kind aviation experience. It was the Coral Route and it helped shape Air New Zealand's destiny. Officially, it was inaugurated on 27 December 1951, but its roots go back further.

In 1942, with World War II well underway and the Pacific an increasingly important focus of the conflict, 1000 Americans and New Zealanders were sent to the remote island of Aitutaki, in the Cook Islands group, to build an airstrip that would serve military purposes. With its waters reflecting shimmering shades of turquoise, emerald and sapphire, Aitutaki would be the gem in the Coral Route's crown.

The war had another important part to play in the development of the Coral Route. The route, according to the teal. co.nz website, "was first charted in wartime when Sunderland flying boats operated by the Royal New Zealand Air Force kept the far-flung island outposts of the British Empire connected. After the war, thousands of experienced, superbly trained ex-military pilots gave civilian aviation a global shot in the arm. The Southern Hemisphere was no exception. Landing on, but not in, a South Pacific lagoon is anything but languorous. During the war, Kiwi pilots had mastered the art of aeronautical island-hopping. Any pilot who didn't study his tide charts and know his currents, and exactly how much clearance he could count on over the heads of the coral reef, tended to get wet fast."

Since 1947, before the Coral Route proper was established, NAC had been operating a fortnightly service from Auckland to Fiji, Samoa, Aitutaki and Rarotonga. When TEAL took over this route it was deemed desirable to add Papeete to it. As the French outpost had no suitable airstrip, flying boats were used instead and the Coral Route was born. Samoa was added as a destination in 1952.

The closest equivalent to the Coral Route today is a Pacific cruise on ocean liner, travelling at a decorous pace from island to island. Very few travellers took the Coral Route, with its short stops at idyllic tropical destinations, for business reasons. It was all about tourism at a time when the concept of tourism – especially airborne tourism – was still in its infancy.

Yet the route had a sound commercial basis. Developing a presence in the Pacific gave people a reason to come this far around the world from major population centres in Europe and the US. A few might have wanted to come to New Zealand for its own sake, but many more would come if there were beautiful Pacific islands, previously out of reach of all but the most intrepid traveller, to enjoy along the way.

TEAL's general manager, Sir Geoffrey Roberts, saw that it was in New Zealand's interest to take a lead in the Pacific. He set his sights on Singapore, Hong Kong, Tokyo, Los Angeles "and if I had my way, Rio". He also saw that such a strategy would build up a fund of goodwill within the Pacific. Before Pacific nations developed their own airlines, with varying degrees of success, Air New Zealand was effectively the Pacific's national airline.

The route's sobriquet was the brainchild of head steward Eric Mullane, who won a competition to name it. He had been so impressed by mass singing at one of the stops that his entry suggested the alternatives Choral or Coral would be equally appropriate. The flights, with a crew of five including a chef providing silver service-standard hospitality to 45 passengers, were a hit from the start. Within just six months the monthly service was doubled to fortnightly.

Captain Nobby Clark was a member of the crew on the first flight. He recalls the Coral Route experience vividly: "The trip was Auckland to Suva, then next morning to Samoa where we stayed at Aggie Gray's hotel, leaving about midnight to fly to Aitutaki. We'd have breakfast and refuel out of the 40-gallon drums. Everyone had a swim and we had breakfast there.

Above far left A sign for TEAL's Hibiscus flight to Auckland.

Above, right and left TEAL buffet lists were mini works of art.

Above left Brochure advertising Fiji shows local food vendors steering canoes laden with fruit.

The Coral Route

6½ HOURS BY
TEAL SOLENT

Aitutaki is a big reef and this was on the south side. They had blasted coral heads to make water runways, so to speak. There was a bure on this island – but it was only occupied when the boat came in once a fortnight (later once a week).

"Another regular part of the trip was that people would get their mail off the flying boat, they could action it and then we'd take their replies back.

"In one case, coming back to Samoa overnight before flying back to Suva the next morning, there was an American couple. He was the boss of a large company and she was a nightmare. Nothing suited her at all. We got back to Samoa, and that night the second steward got bitten by a dog. Going out to the plane in the bus, the captain explained to the passengers what had happened, and said that the steward was no use for anything. And when it came time for lunch service on the flight, this woman leapt in and became second hostess and couldn't have been happier."

Navigating such wide expanses of open sea and sky required a great deal of skill, without the assistance of modern technological navigation equipment. Even at that time aircraft tended to rely on ground-based radio assistance to find their way, but this was scarce in the Pacific. "Position finding was largely done by astro fixes," says author Neil Rennie, "with the navigator shooting sun lines by day and stars at night. He used a periscopic sextant which was extended through an aperture in the top of the fuselage."

It required a lot of such work to create this relaxing experience. Infinite pains were taken to ensure that reality did not intrude into the travellers' South Sea Island fantasy. Frank Reeves, later general manager of TEAL, remembers siting the passenger-handling building and fuel dumps behind coconut trees so they couldn't be seen. When Americans stepped ashore, "they felt they were stepping into nothing".

Nothing, in fact, could be further from the truth – much went on behind the scenes. Refuelling in such remote locations was a complicated part of the exercise.

According to one source: "The fuel for the Solents, which was pumped by hand from the jetty into the flying boat's tanks, made its journey there in a manner almost as laboured as the plane's. It was taken by sea from New Zealand to Aitutaki, where the tanker stood off the passage at Arutanga (Aitutaki's port), on the western side of the main island. From the tanker, drums of fuel were unloaded by lighter (a smaller barge-like vessel) and taken to Arutanga wharf, and thence by boat around the southern end of the main island and across the wide lagoon to the wharf on Akaiami, to await the arrival (on Thursdays) of the thirsty Solent and its 45 passengers."

The passengers lived up to the image of their journey, reflecting back the glamour of the trip. "It was the first time I'd seen American women with blue-rinsed hair," recalls a former flight attendant. "They wore things like nets with butterfly things on to keep their hair in place. They were lovely. It was glamorous."

One story enshrined in Coral Route legend is that of the occasion on which the plane suffered an engine malfunction coming into Aitutaki. There being no engineering workshop on Aitutaki – that was the point, after all – the captain had to take the plane off for repairs. He unloaded passengers, crew, food, blankets and other supplies and disappeared into the sky. The travellers were muttering to the point of mutiny, but there was no alternative. Unfortunately, the distance involved and the time the repairs took meant the plane did not return for its charges for eight days. In the interim, they had become thoroughly conditioned to life on a tropical island, and it was with some difficulty that the full complement was persuaded back on board.

Eventually competition, costs and a growing sophistication in tourism in other destinations meant that the Coral Route had reached the end of its useful life. In 1960, the last Solent was taken off the Coral Route, ending the world's last scheduled international flying-boat service.

Above left Welcoming party for TEAL passengers, Papeete, Tahiti, 1952.

Above Coral Route crew members at Akaiami, Aitutaki, Cook Islands, 1952.

Right Locals on the beach at Akaiami, Aitutaki, in the Cook Islands. A sailboat and TEAL flying boat rest in the water.

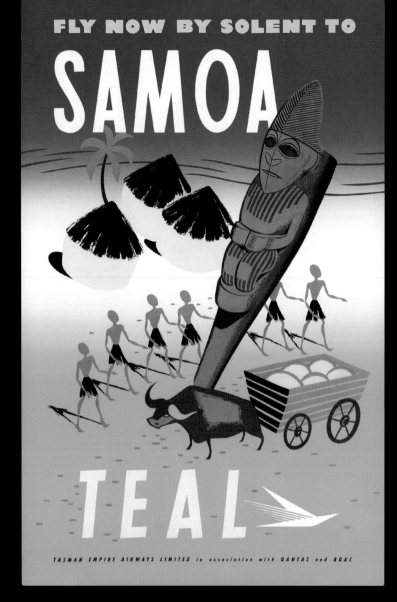

Pacific promises

The stylised imagery of TEAL's early advertising posters painted an idyllic picture of the Pacific, and cleverly incorporated the airline's corporate logos.

fiji BY AIR BY *TEAL*

RESTFUL
NORFOLK ISLAND

FLY TEAL

TEAL

MAN EMPIRE AIRWAYS LTD.

EAL

ZK-AML

Regal pedigree

Opposite A young Queen Elizabeth II undertook an antipodean tour of the Empire in 1954 accompanied by Prince Philip. They departed Fiji for New Zealand on *Aotearoa II*.

Below Queen Elizabeth and Prince Philip thank the Air New Zealand crew at Perth airport after a short visit to New Zealand in October 1951.

Bottom The Queen Mother arrives on the *Britannia* at Whenuapai, Auckland, 1958.

When it comes to the royal treatment, Air New Zealand has always been right up there – from Queen Elizabeth's first flight on a commercial airliner to the day Prince Philip himself took the controls.

Air New Zealand has had a long-standing association with the royal family, one that is nearly as old as the airline itself.

It goes back to the christening of TEAL's Solent flying boat flagship, ZK-AML *Aotearoa II*, which was performed by the then-Princess Elizabeth in Belfast in 1949. Reflecting shared loyalties, it was delivered with the New Zealand flag on one side of the tail fins and the Union Jack on the other. (A veil should perhaps be drawn over the fact that the Queen used a bottle of Australian wine to perform the christening.) Before the ceremony the aircraft's name, painted on the side, was covered with a Union Jack, which fell away to reveal the name once the bottle had been smashed on its side.

A few years later, now Queen Elizabeth II, the monarch embarked on a tour of the Pacific with her husband, Prince Philip. This had a substantial TEAL component. The Queen got to sample a stretch of the Coral Route, flying from Suva to Lautoka and Tonga on a Solent flying boat: this was the first

flight on a commercial airliner by members of the royal family.

Captain Nobby Clark was on this flight as navigator, replacing the rostered crew member at the last minute. He recalls that for such a momentous event, the whole trip was rehearsed beforehand. "Everything before we started – the times each step of the trip took, for instance. The Solent was fitted out specially for royalty. At the end of our leg of the trip, we took the couple to Tonga where they joined the royal yacht *Britannia* for the rest of their journey."

A great number of British reporters had been sent to follow the young queen on this early tour. Because they were so far from their news desks, they would write stories in advance, file them when they could and then give instructions to print them at the appropriate times. There was much generic describing of palm trees and azure waters.

"We were set to come back having safely delivered the Queen and Duke," recalls Clark, "and we lost an engine on

Clockwise from above
The royal cabin on
ZK-NZE, 1974.

Princess Alexandra
greets Air New
Zealand crew after
the purchase of TEAL
whose Southern Cross
still forms part of the
company logo.

A soup tureen from
the gold-plated dinner
service TEAL had made
for the Royal tour.

Princess Elizabeth with
the Duke of Edinburgh,
alighting from aircraft
Aotearoa, June 1949.

take-off. So we unloaded everybody. We couldn't take the reporters on our three engines. They weren't happy but there was nothing we could do. In fact, the company took a Mark IV flying boat off the Tasman route at the busiest time of the year and sent it to Tonga to rescue the reporters. Needless to say, it wasn't as comfortable as the royal aircraft.

"Our first job was to fly the royal couple from Suva to Lautoka – they went ashore and we had to stay on the plane, which was hot. They continued around the island and overflew a leper colony. We had just got started on that flight when the Duke arrived on the flight deck. He's a pilot in his own right so he got in the right-hand seat and he flew the aeroplane around the island. No problem. The next day the Queen arrived on the flight deck. Word came that she was coming up and we were ordered to 'smarten up'. Since she had to climb stairs to get to the flight deck, there was also an order that there would be no looking up royal skirts."

In January 1954, the Queen and Prince Philip flew from Rotorua to Gisborne on an NAC Heron. Twenty years later, the Queen, accompanied by Princess Anne and her husband, Mark Phillips, flew to New Zealand on an Air New Zealand DC-8 to close the Commonwealth Games. On the way Her Majesty stopped in the Cook Islands to officially open the new Rarotonga International Airport.

Numerous other flights followed during royal tours over the years, but the next royal landmark flight came in 1995, when the Queen flew in an Air New Zealand 747 on NZ1 from Los Angeles to Auckland to attend the Commonwealth Heads of Government Meeting. This was the first time that a reigning monarch had flown on a scheduled commercial flight. "This was a great honour," recalls an executive who was involved in the arrangements. "Royalty already had a big record of travelling with Air New Zealand, but every other flight was chartered or an air force flight."

It may have been a regular flight but there was nothing routine about the arrangements that had to be made. "It was a huge logistical exercise, from working with officials in Buckingham Palace, to getting various agreements. A lot of people were involved in the planning, including the flight operations people and the captain himself. There had to be special security measures and clearances for everyone involved.

"The first class area was taken out completely and a new cabin put in. We installed a couple of armchairs, a desk, a dressing room and a signing table. She flew from London to Auckland and back and it was a huge exercise in each direction."

Right and below
The Queen visits Sri Lanka at the end of her Australasian tour in 1981. After she had removed her shoes to enter a Buddhist temple, Her Majesty's aides realised she had nothing to cover her feet. The day was saved when a pair of Air New Zealand socks were produced.

Official opening of Wellington Airport

24 October 1959

Above left People gather on the tarmac to witness the airport's official opening.

Top Eager spectators brave the Wellington weather, looking on from a bank.

Above The official opening event inside the terminal, complete with banquet table.

Top left Cars park to avoid the puddles.

Above left An aerial view of Wellington Airport.

Top middle The crowd queues for a close-up look at the aircraft.

Above middle *Evening Post* reporter Scott Francis on seating constructed for the opening.

Top right Kiwis young and old came out to witness the occasion.

Above right The crowd leaves after the event is postponed due to bad weather.

Ed in the clouds

History-making explorer Sir Edmund Hillary began and ended many a journey climbing aboard an aircraft. After his successful ascent of Mount Everest, and his subsequent knighthood, TEAL was there to bring him home.

One great New Zealand institution deserves another, and Air New Zealand had a long association with Everest conqueror, humanitarian and adventurer Sir Edmund Hillary.

It was a TEAL Solent that brought Hillary back to his home town and a hero's welcome following the ascent of Everest. He reached the summit in May 1953, but the mountaineer didn't reach Auckland again until August. He had come home the long way, stopping to be knighted by the Queen and feted wherever he went.

For most New Zealanders outside the climbing fraternity, their first sight of Ed Hillary in person was when he alighted from the flying boat at Mechanics Bay. For TEAL, the newsreel must have been a public relations dream come true.

The link was maintained over the years. One of history's great travellers, Hillary was always either planning, preparing or departing on a journey, and Air New Zealand figured largely in those plans.

Norm Thompson, later deputy chief executive of Air New Zealand, was a booking officer in the early days of his career, and Hillary was a regular customer. "He'd come in with his backpack and sit down," recalls Thompson. "A lovely man who always had difficult itineraries because he was going to Kathmandu in Nepal. Trying to get him an easy route to those places was always difficult."

With no instant access to airline routes and timetables, Thompson and Hillary had to rely on the voluminous Official Airline Guide to plan his trips. "Phone calls would have been too difficult," says Thompson. "So you'd book Ed Auckland to Singapore, Singapore to Bombay, Bombay to Kathmandu. You'd work out an itinerary and put in your reservation, but you had to wait a week or 10 days for confirmation of the sectors. The answer used to come via telex.

"At the Kathmandu end, things were a lot more basic than they were here, and you had to wait for ages. And the delay meant you could have travel times at each end confirmed, but then the one in the middle might fall out and you'd have to start all over again."

Women in uniforms

Taking their cue from the industry's air force origins, early crew uniforms were the height of flight sophistication, but changing fashions and duties meant updates were on the horizon.

Left The original six TEAL stewardesses in the first uniform, 1946.

Top Modelling the summer uniform at Mechanics Bay, 1947.

Above A Solent stewardess leaves an aircraft at Mechanics Bay, 1950.

It's not entirely clear why air crew uniforms so fascinate people, but there's no doubt they do. Perhaps it's because uniforms are such a big part of the company's image. Perhaps it's because as garments they are unlike any other kind of wardrobe. Whatever the reason, every time a new uniform is introduced, it's national news and the merits of the new design are hotly debated.

Changing uniforms is not something that is undertaken lightly – for one thing, it's estimated that issuing a new set now costs the company around $2 million. But changing job requirements and the march of fashion dictate that uniforms must be updated regularly.

Originally uniforms reflected the air force origins of so much civil aviation tradition. Until the introduction of the Dior uniform in 1961, TEAL uniforms from 1946-50 were in military style with all the trimmings.

"They were very tailored," recalls one hostess who flew the Coral Route. "The dress uniform in winter was black with a white shirt and black tie. They were made by David Jones in Sydney and were very fitted. When you took them off you could see the shape of a bosom, waist and hips in the clothes. We had black shoes, handbag and gloves and cap that we always wore."

Or as the official account has it: "The uniform was in black barathea, made in military style with square-shouldered double-breasted jackets. Man-styled white shirt with ties and Glengarry hats. In summer the uniform was white shirt-waist dresses in fawn gabardine."

There were actually two uniforms. To complicate matters somewhat, crew had to change on the plane.

"The summer dress uniform was like the American marines' one – khaki with a silk shirt, tan tie and shoes, and a beige cap. But on board we wore a white uniform like a nurse's. It was very stiffly starched. As soon as you greeted your passengers, you changed into your whites, then just before landing, you changed into your dress uniform. In a very confined space."

That look was described as "clean, white and clinical".

Child's play

The idea of flying has never fascinated and delighted any group more than the lucky boys and girls who climbed aboard some of New Zealand's earliest aircraft and took to the skies.

Clockwise from top left George Bolt, 1923; a schoolboy talks to the pilot of Solent flying boat *Awatere*, 1951; a group of young plane-spotters in front of a de Havilland DH86 which was the first aircraft to be used by Union Airways; an NAC DC-3 at Whenuapai Airport, 1953.

(70) History: 1960–1969
Milestones and other memorable moments from the decade.

(76) Beatlemania hits New Zealand
The Fab Four touch down in Wellington.

(78) Freight expectations
Aircraft cargo takes many forms.

(80) TEAL turns 21 in style
The airline comes of age.

(81) Stamps of approval
Commemorative first-day covers.

(82) High exposure
Air-to-air photography, then and now.

(84) An air of sophistication
New York's top model takes to the skies.

(86) LA times
An all-American makeover as Los Angeles becomes one of the airline's major destinations.

(88) It's all in the name
Air New Zealand is born.

(90) The way they wore
Dior-designed uniforms are introduced.

(94) The jet set
Entering the jet age, and the arrival of the DC-8.

(98) International arrival
The country's biggest airport opens in Auckland.

(100) Tag team
Retro bag tags.

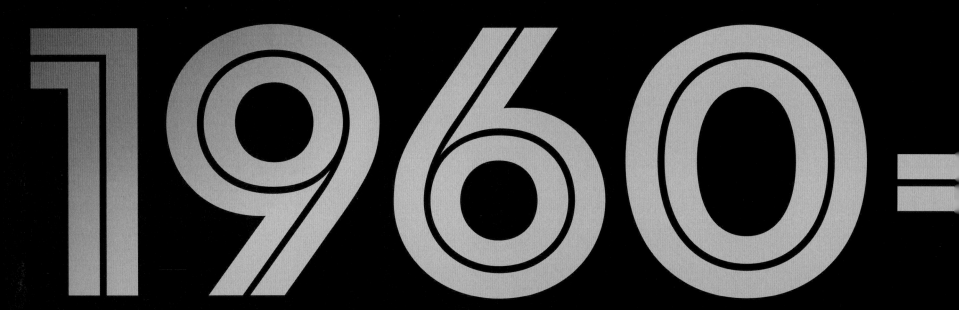

=1969

The 1960s saw TEAL enter the jet age and take on a new name, becoming Air New Zealand in 1965. Both were major shifts, reflecting in one case the development of technology which would transform the international airline industry, and in the other emphasising the company's identification with its home country as a point of pride and a global marketing tool.

With many more international travel choices available and increasingly within reach of the average consumer, the Coral Route had run its course, and it came to an end with a farewell flight in 1960. The following year the Australian government's 50 percent share of TEAL was sold to the New Zealand government, which now owned the airline outright.

By the beginning of the decade NAC had flown five million domestic passengers, demonstrating that flight was now seen as a standard option for anyone wanting to get around the country.

TEAL ordered its first DC-8s in 1963 and two years later began using the first of them on the Christchurch-Sydney service.

On 1 April 1965, at the instigation of the board, TEAL changed its name to Air New Zealand. Expansion was just around the corner and it was necessary to get the name change in place before launching into new markets.

The new generation of jet aircraft was too big to be accommodated by the old airport at Whenuapai. When the new Auckland International Airport was built at Mangere – a relatively small one-building domestic and international terminal combined – its first outward bound craft was a DC-8 to Sydney. The following month, a DC-8 took off for Los Angeles, via Tahiti, inaugurating a route which would remain crucial to the airline's business. Hong Kong, Brisbane and Singapore were soon added to the company's destinations.

The airline also raised its global profile throughout the decade with a programme of increased representation, opening offices in centres around the world.

By the beginning of the decade NAC had flown five million domestic passengers, demonstrating that flight was now seen as a standard option for anyone wanting to get around the country.

Above The Beatles were among many celebrities brought to New Zealand by TEAL in the 1960s, but none drew crowds the size of those who turned out to meet the group.

Left A passenger with her guide dog aboard a DC-8.

Above right Air New Zealand enters the Hong Kong market with a hiss and a roar.

Right An exciting new route called for a cocktail and a chance to shout about Air New Zealand's superlative service standards.

Far right After 20 years of loyal service, the last of the Solents were retired. ZK-AMO *Aranui* can now be found at Auckland's Museum of Transport and Technology.

11 July 1960
TEAL information and sales office opens in Sydney.

September 1960
Five million domestic passengers carried by NAC since 1947.

15 September 1960
Return of last Solent, ZK-AMO *Aranui*, to Auckland after a farewell flight over the 7402km Coral Route.

December 1960
First Fokker F27 Friendship, ZK-BXA, arrives in Wellington.

Top and top right TEAL's information and sales office opens in Sydney, taking the airline's business to its customers.

Right Air New Zealand flies "Old Blue" – a casting of a champion marlin caught in the Bay of Islands – to the Los Angeles Sportsman Vacation and Travel Show, 1968.

HISTORICAL EVENTS IN NEW ZEALAND
1960–69

1960
- Regular TV programmes introduced in Auckland (left).
- Treasury leases New Zealand's first computer from IBM.

- *A Good Keen Man* by Barry Crump is published (right).

1961
- New Zealand joins the International Monetary Fund.
- Capital punishment abolished for the second time.
- Golden Kiwi lottery launched (right).

28 April 1961

The Minister of Civil Aviation, J.K. McAlpine, announces New Zealand will purchase Australia's half share in TEAL. The two governments decide that Australia's Qantas will receive trans-Tasman rights.

30 April 1961

TEAL's 21st anniversary. Birthday cake is served on board all seven flights airborne that day.

January 1962

Trans-Tasman flights reach a record 33 return services weekly.

March 1962

100,000 tonnes of freight/mail carried on domestic network.

6 September 1962

Record crossing of the Tasman by a jet-prop Electra, in two hours 52 minutes.

3 July 1963

An NAC DC-3, ZK-AYZ, crashes in the Kaimai Ranges with the loss of 23 passengers and crew.

23 September 1963

Contract signed with the Douglas Aircraft Company for the purchase of three DC-8 jets.

Top right The DC-3, ZK-AYZ, had survived flying in World War II, only to perish in the Kaimai Ranges.

Bottom right The crash site lay deep in almost impenetrable bush.

Far right, top A rescue crew sets out for the crash site. It took two days to reach the wreckage.

Far right, bottom Assessing the damage.

1962
- Troops sent to Malaysia during confrontation with Indonesia.
- Western Samoa becomes independent.

- Sir Guy Powles (right) becomes first Ombudsman.
- Taranaki gas well opens.
- Peter Snell breaks world mile record running in Whanganui (far right).

- Maurice Wilkins shares the Nobel Prize for medicine with Watson and Crick for his part in the discovery of DNA.

1963
- Death of pioneer aviator George Bolt (left), who took New Zealand's first aerial photographs in 1912 and delivered its first official airmail in 1919.

1960–1969

1 April 1965
TEAL changes its name to Air New Zealand.

20 July 1965
Arrival of first DC-8, ZK-NZA, after a 6510-mile, nonstop flight from Long Beach, California to Auckland. The flight took 13 hours and 32 minutes, with an average speed of 530mph.

24 November 1965
First commercial services through new Auckland International Airport. An Electra from Nadi is the first international arrival; a DC-8 to Sydney is the first departure.

29 January 1966
Official opening of the new Auckland International Airport at Mangere is marked with a three-day pageant.

3 March 1966
First DC-8 Auckland-Hong Kong commercial service.

Right Air New Zealand Crown Lynn pottery from 1965, now sought after by collectors and museums.

Below The airline's first DC-8 arrives at a time of transition and carries the names TEAL and Air New Zealand.

1965
- NAFTA (free trade) agreement negotiated with Australia.
- Support for United States in Vietnam; New Zealand combat force sent; protest movement begins.
- Riots at Auckland's Mt Eden Prison (right).

1966
- New Zealand labour force reaches one million.
- National Library of New Zealand created.
- Te Atairangi Kaahu becomes first Maori Queen (right).
- Pirate/private station Radio Hauraki begins transmission.

May 1966
Ten millionth passenger carried on NAC's domestic network.

4 July 1966
DC-8 ZK-NZB crashes during a training flight to Auckland. Two crew killed.

10 May 1967
Air New Zealand office opens in London.

October 1967
Air New Zealand purchases a 20 percent shareholding in Polynesian Airlines Limited.

5 November 1967
Air New Zealand resumes services to Tahiti, following termination of rights in 1964. The Auckland-Tahiti sector will become the first leg of a new route to Los Angeles.

31 July 1968
Cook Islands Airways Limited formed with all shares held by Air New Zealand.

September-October 1968
First three Boeing 737-200 aircraft arrive.

11 September 1968
On the 40th anniversary of Charles Kingsford Smith's epic trans-Tasman flight, an Air New Zealand DC-8 carries radio operator T.H. McWilliams as a passenger on an Auckland-Sydney service. The DC-8 is piloted by Captain R. McWilliams, son of the VIP passenger.

1967
• 10 July: Decimal currency introduced (right).

• Aviator Fred Ladd illegally flies his amphibian aircraft under Auckland Harbour Bridge.

• Lord Arthur Porritt becomes first New Zealand-born Governor-General (left).

• Free milk in schools programme ends.

1968
• Inter-island ferry *Wahine* sinks in severe storm in Wellington Harbour (left); 51 people killed.

Beatlemania hits New Zealand

21 June 1964

No group or person had ever received such a welcome in New Zealand as the one that erupted when the Beatles stepped out of a TEAL aircraft at Wellington Airport in 1964. The ensuing tour was to become one of the defining events of the decade.

This page Paul, Ringo, John and George touch down in the capital.

Opposite page, top row, from left The crowd at Wellington Airport, awaiting the arrival of the Beatles.

Ringo, John and Paul try their hand at poi, while George chats with a member of the welcome party.

Opposite page, bottom row, from left Ringo receives a traditional hongi as George and TEAL crew look on.

Ringo (left) and George during the tour of New Zealand.

Freight expectations

Left Livestock might fly – a truck backs up to load a Bristol Freighter at Hood Aerodrome, Masterton.

Top Air New Zealand took the inter-island ferries head on with its offer to fly passengers and their cars across Cook Strait.

Above Loading freight into the side of a DC8 freighter.

Air New Zealand has several revenue streams – as well as passengers, there's also mail, contracted services such as engineering, and freight, which can be anything from fresh vegetables and frozen food to live bees.

Carrying freight as well as passengers and mail was an important part of NAC's and TEAL's operations from the start.

Air freight revolutionised global business in the 20th century. Not only could goods be speedily moved around the world – enabling more fresh food items, for instance, to be exported – but it also removed the need for conventional warehousing as goods no longer needed to be stored for lengthy periods before being delivered to their markets.

In the Coral Route days, for instance, a former US marine who was living on Aitutaki found it worth his while to grow tomatoes for export to Tahiti.

Thanks to air freight, any item was no more than 36 hours from anywhere in the world, although the trade was at first mainly in high-value, low-bulk goods which cost less to carry. An NAC DC-3 could hold up to three tonnes of freight if used just as a freighter. The 1965 DC-8 could carry seven tonnes of cargo – which was equivalent to the total amount carried by TEAL in its first year.

During the 1951 waterfront strike, which threatened to bring the national economy to a standstill as ships were prevented from carrying freight, the TEAL cargo business quadrupled to 647 tonnes compared to the year before.

In 1961 an Electra flew the first chilled fish to Australia. Chilled meat was flown to Hong Kong and Singapore the following year. In 1963 the first racehorses were flown across the Tasman, and the horse trade between New Zealand and Australia, mainly for breeding, although occasionally for racing, has been a thriving form of commerce ever since.

Between 1964 and 1984, passenger numbers increased by a healthy 77.5 percent, but the cargo arm of the business increased by a spectacular 2000 percent.

With the arrival of the big jets, the air freight business was transformed yet again. DC-10s ushered in the container era and the cargo business experienced another surge of growth.

TEAL turns 21 in style

The airline had come a long way in its first 21 years, and celebrated with a variety of special events and activities, including birthday cake for everyone who flew on 30 April.

Below left A birthday key ring.

Below The front page of the *New Zealand Herald* special supplement.

Right TEAL's lively staff magazine had much to talk about when the company turned 21.

TEAL's 21st Anniversary
ZK-AMA
1940
Supplement to THE NEW ZEALAND HERALD
1961

TEALAGRAM

PUBLISHED MONTHLY

VOLUME 4 **APRIL-MAY 1961** **NUMBER 12**

WE COME OF AGE

21 Years of Operation for N.Z.'s International Airline

GRAPHIC RECORD OF COMPANY'S GROWTH

This comparison of figures, taken over a period of 21 years, shows graphically how much we have advanced. "T/T" single trips refers, of course, to trans-Tasman. You will note from 1951, that the first and second columns differ, due to our increase in routes—Wellington, Fiji and the Coral Route adding to both mileage, flights and passenger figures.

Year Ending	T/T Single Trips	Total No. of Single Trips T/T	Fax. Total Pax
31/3/41	130	130	1,461
31/3/42	158	158	1,977
31/3/43	144	144	2,256
31/3/44	164	164	2,850
31/3/45	319	319	5,850
31/3/46	365	365	6,111
31/3/47	581	581	11,648
31/3/48	752	752	19,245
31/3/49	876	876	24,522 c/Fwd
31/3/50	881	881	22,579 98,499
31/3/51	897	983	29,057 31,233
31/3/52	1,215	1,324	39,317 42,301
31/3/53	1,085	1,225	32,999 36,898
31/3/54	975	1,122	30,888 35,910
31/3/55	927	1,274	35,398 43,644
31/3/56	1,039	1,388	41,001 50,864
31/3/57	1,147	1,553	49,489 62,159
31/3/58	1,178	1,567	48,679 62,127
31/3/59	1,321	1,726	53,205 67,438
31/3/60	1,358	1,718	61,671 76,405
Total first 20 years	15,512	18,250	520,203 607,478
Y/E 31/3/61	1,666	2,115	88,181 103,382
Estimated month April 1961	148	182	7,875 9,175
Total 21 years to 30/4/61	17,326	20,547	616,259 720,035

If over 900 people joined together in riotous song "We've got the key of the door — never been 21 before", we'd probably be picked up for being disorderly. Being a dignified company with the impressive title of "New Zealand's International Airline", we'll be less boisterous but none the less gay. Let's shout it to the world.

We are 21. It is no mean achievement.

The mums and dads among us know the responsibility, the heartaches and the laughs of guiding one's young to the ripe old age of maturity. The same applies to the gallant band of TEALERS, from the General Manager down to the first apprentice, who with high courage, faith and perseverance (and laughs) created and guided an airline, TEAL, until today it holds a position of respect throughout the world.

TEAL is the airline of the South Pacific. We have come up from a 19 passenger carrying airline to jet-prop speed carrying 70 passengers at a time. Our economy is healthy: in fact, as a major aviation concern reported to the world only a year ago, we "bristle with wisdom".

Happy birthday, TEALERS.

Sunday, 30th April marks the anniversary of TEAL's — and New Zealand's — commercial passenger service, when an S.30 flying-boat flew from Auckland to Sydney with 10 passengers and a crew under the command of Captain J. W. Burgess.

During our 21 years of operation, services and traffic have grown with the growth of international aviation. We progressed from original S.30 flyingboats to Sandringhams and Solents, to DC-6's and now jet-prop Electras.

Each successive generation of aircraft represented increases in speed, engine power, technical advancement; but, more important, the capacity to carry the ever-growing flow of international air traffic through the South Pacific.

By the time we reached 10 years of age in 1950, routes had been extended to take in Wellington, Christchurch and Fiji. In the following year, routes were extended further — along the Coral Route to Tahiti.

In 21 years of operation, route network has grown from 1,300 to 13,000. Passenger traffic has grown 70-fold from an annual rate of 1461 to 103,382.

In our first year of operation, we flew 130 trans-Tasman crossings and carried 1,462 passengers. Figures have grown progressively through the years so that, in this year ending 31st March last, we flew 1666 trans-Tasman crossings and carried 88,181 passengers on trans-Tasman routes.

Throughout the 21 years to April 30, 1961, we will have flown 20,546 services over all routes and carried a total, including traffic estimated to end of April, of 720,035.

We have earned profits in 17 of these years, totalling £N.Z. 1.57 million, as against incurring losses in four years of £N.Z. .57 million, leaving a net earned surplus of £NZ 1 million. Over the past five years, the annual average profit has been £N.Z. 225,000 per year.

ANNUAL BALL

Feature motif of this year's annual ball will be TEAL's 21st anniversary. Generous assistance from management will help make this function bigger and brighter than ever. There'll be a champagne toast and a fabulous floor show.

The Sports, Social and Welfare Committee is anxious to make this a real TEAL staff ball and, accordingly, have reduced the subscription to £2. 2. 0. per double ticket for financial members of the club.

We can't tell you all the good news about it — come and see. Good dancing, the usual excellent supper — and lots of wonderful surprise items. This is OUR birthday year — and only YOU can help add to the gaiety and joy of such an historic occasion.

You can buy tickets from April 17 to May 1. And, don't get lazy — the TEAL BALL is on Friday, 12th May at the Peter Pan Cabaret, Queen Street.

Our General Manager, Mr. Reeves, writes "Well done" on our latest passenger record board in the Airways House cafeteria.

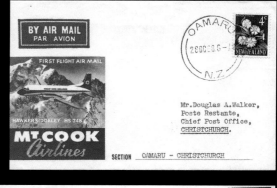

Stamps of approval

First-day covers commemorate special flights of NAC, TEAL and Air New Zealand aircraft, as well as the opening of Auckland International Airport.

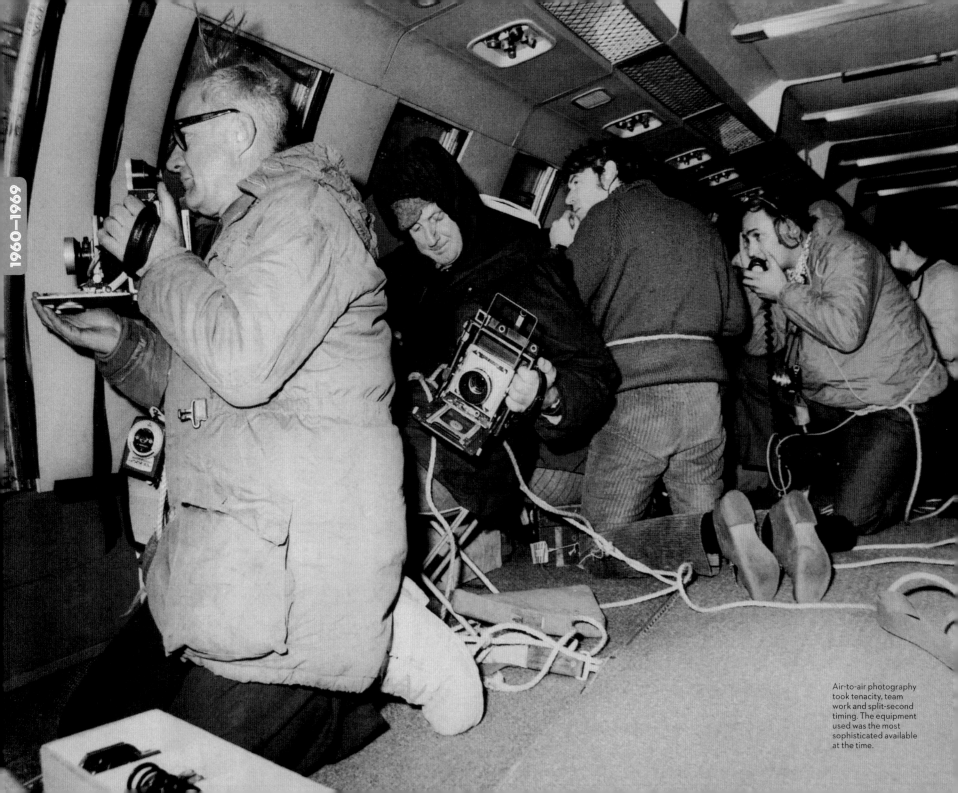

Air-to-air photography took tenacity, team work and split-second timing. The equipment used was the most sophisticated available at the time.

High exposure

Shots of aircraft in flight are iconic aviation images. The early pioneers of air-to-air photography were innovative, courageous... and cold.

It's the sort of thing you don't think about unless you're involved, but every time you see a photo of an aircraft shot against a spectacular backdrop, it means someone in another aircraft with a camera has worked very hard to get that shot.

Air-to-air photography has changed considerably since the early days. One of the pioneers of the art form was the airline's Richard Williams, doyen of Air New Zealand PR men.

"In August 1962," says Williams, "management wanted aircraft photos for promotional material. Some good photos had been lost in a fire at head office so they were badly needed. Also a livery change meant a lot of the old photos were out of date in the international era."

He contacted Guy Mannering and Pat Dolan from Mannering and Associates, whose work for NAC engineering included spectacular shots over Mount Cook. "We needed large-format colour negative and positive, and they used 5x4-inch cameras with lenses slightly wider than normal to provide pleasing perspective. We also invited National Film Unit cameramen to take 35mm film for stock use."

Williams decided to photograph the aircraft against some of New Zealand's most spectacular backgrounds – the mountains, lakes and glaciers of the South Island. After all, these would be showing off the country as a destination, as well as promoting the aircraft as a means of reaching the destination, here and overseas, in newspapers and magazines as well as point-of-sale displays, TV ads and inflight magazines.

For his forays, he planned a route from Christchurch to Mount Arrowsmith to Mount Tasman, the Tasman Glacier, Mount Cook, Mount Sefton, Lake Ohau, Benmore, Timaru, Ashburton, Banks Peninsula and Christchurch city. "We flew at up to 10,000ft in the Mount Cook region to get the best scale."

A simple solution was found to overcome the problem of reflections from the aeroplane windows at the camera end – they were removed, along with some emergency escape hatches. "For communication between pilots I had a microphone and earphones to co-ordinate manoeuvres along the route and relay progress to the cameraman. Sometimes we did circuits over landmarks to get variety."

Filming without windows was noisy and cold, but any discomfort was forgotten in the excitement of flying in close formation against spectacular landscapes. Williams would warn Mount Cook National Park rangers that two aircraft would be flying low over their mountains so they could alert climbers. One of the more memorable moments on one flight came when those in the air saw huge avalanches coming off Mount Tasman and Mount Elie de Beaumont. Another time, when they were flying over South Canterbury, a concerned observer rang the authorities to report that two planes appeared to be in trouble and were flying together in an unusual way.

Not all the important photography took place in the air however – there were also spectacular shots to be had from the ground, albeit in occasionally hair-raising circumstances. "I used to do filming at the airport," says Williams. "I'd go out on the runway to shoot a 747 taking off. I'd be right beside the runway – Civil Aviation let us do that then – and we'd talk to the pilot: 'Where are you going to lift off so we can get that moment with the wheels?' Or, 'We want you to land 1000ft down the runway so we can get a nice greasy [smooth] landing, not bumpy as some pilots still do.' "

The early experiments and subsequent flights were a great success and brought home some of the best-known images in Air New Zealand's history.

Above Every new livery meant new air-to-air shots were required. Cameras mounted on the front of helicopters make the job a lot easier these days.

Handmacher Flies the Coral Route...to New Zealand

An air of sophistication

TEAL turned heads in 1963 when it featured in American *Vogue* magazine in a giant promotion of the Coral Route to launch US fashion house Handmacher's new "Coral Line" of women's clothing. To show off the garments "in South Seas settings" TEAL flew top New York model of the day, Margot McKendry, and a production crew around New Zealand and the islands of the Coral Route on a two-week trip.

Left A fashion shoot on Mount Cook featured in American *Vogue*.

Right The Coral Route tour visited top tourist resorts in Tahiti, Samoa and Fiji.

Handmacher
Flies the
Coral Route
...to Fiji

TEAL

E893

Handmacher Flies the Coral Route...to Tahiti

TEAL

Handmacher Flies the Coral Route...to the South Seas

TEAL

LA times

Soon after the first DC-8 flight there, in 1965, Los Angeles became one of the airline's major routes. By the mid-1990s, Air New Zealand was the biggest foreign carrier flying into LA.

Top left Kiri Te Kanawa (not yet Dame Kiri) helped with a musical launch for flights to the entertainment capital.

Above Air New Zealand goes all-American.

LOS ANGELES

HAWAII

FIJI

AUCKLAND

SYDNEY
MELBOURNE•
BRISBANE•

AIR NEW ZEALAND

Now to LOS ANGELES and soon to HONG KONG

Already twice weekly to Los Angeles! And now, from 3rd March, twice weekly to Hong Kong! Air New Zealand's giant new DC-8's with Five Star Jetline service *all* the way. Book your U.S.A. or Orient bound clients Air New Zealand — they'll thank *you* for it always. Full scheduling information from AIR NEW ZEALAND in Sydney (28-2786). Melbourne (63-2554). Brisbane (31-2548).

*Melbourne/Auckland and Brisbane/Auckland sectors operated by International Electras

AIR NEW ZEALAND
The Five Star Jetline *in association with QANTAS and BOAC*

11200

AP57.147.85Sc

FIVE EXOTIC WAYS TO ENJOY YOUR BUSINESS TRIP TO AND FROM THE USA.

air new zealand

NOW EVERY DAY TO THE USA AIR NEW ZEALAND'S ROLLS ROYCE BOEING 747 SUPER B's

SYD/AKL/HNL/LAX

air new zealand

ONE OF THE SERVICES WE OFFER YOU 10 TIMES A WEEK TO LOS ANGELES.

The Pacific's Number One
air new zealand

'FREEDOM FARES' TO THE USA GIVE YOU 5 PACIFIC STOPOVERS.

HAWAII
TAHITI
RAROTONGA
NEW ZEALAND
FIJI

air new zealand

Just that much better.

DAILY 747 FLIGHTS

air new zealand

Fly the flag
The Pacific's Number One
air new zealand

NEW LOW FARES ANNOUNCED!

Auckland-Los Angeles $458 return!*
Auckland-Honolulu $416 return!*

Your Airline
air new zealand

Below Both TEAL and Air New Zealand appeared for a short time on the livery after the name change. TEAL Managing Director of the time, Sir Geoffrey Roberts, second from right.

Right The name change filtered through to all aspects of the business. The staff magazine *TEALagram* could no longer be, and gave way to *The Air New Zealander.*

The AIR NEW ZEALANDER

PUBLISHED MONTHLY

| VOLUME 1 | APRIL 1965 | NUMBER 1 |

AIR NEW ZEALAND
AIR NEW ZEALAND
AIR NEW ZEALAND
AIR NEW ZEALAND
AIR NEW ZEALAND
AIR NEW ZEALAND

This is the first issue of The AIR NEW ZEALANDER — successor to the staff magazine TEALAGRAM which TEAL began publishing ten years ago.

This first issue, of course, is published to coincide with the company's name change to AIR NEW ZEALAND from April 1 and we take the opportunity to seek a wider audience than the company's staff alone. Therefore the first issue is being distributed to our agents and associates and to the Press.

In it we highlight our name change and explain just how we are making the change. We show the new type face we have developed for AIR NEW ZEALAND (that's it on the left). And above we show the biggest, most dramatic symbol of the change — a photograph of our first DC8 taking off at Long Beach, California, on a certification flight (these DC8's incorporate advanced developments which require re-certification).

The DC8 is a symbol and a vehicle too. It is the vehicle which will enable AIR NEW ZEALAND to take this country's name into America and Asia, as well as along the South Pacific routes TEAL has been serving for 25 years.

In this broader field we will match our service of the past and seek to improve it. We will maintain the concept of personal service to our passengers so that our airline, in association with its Commonwealth partners, will continue to be a bridge of understanding and of trade between the nations that we serve.

We will make New Zealand better known overseas and will bring increasing numbers of people to visit this country. We have a job to do for New Zealand and, with the DC8's, we will be equipped to do it.

It's all in the name

Tahitian Entertainer?

Terrifically Exciting?

The world and the aviation industry were changing. Poised to take off in bold new directions, those in charge of TEAL decided that a new name was called for – one that said something about who the airline was.

In its silver anniversary year, 1965, TEAL became Air New Zealand. Given that an airline's home nation has a lot to do with where it can fly and conveys to customers a good deal of what they can expect from the carrier, it makes sense to include it in the name, as many national airlines do. The name change and timing had come at the request of the board. They could see not only that it was inevitable but also that a period of expansion into new markets was fast approaching and that it was essential to go in with a name that would not soon be altered.

"This change has been brought about by the very practical need to identify the airline more closely with New Zealand in the wider international aviation scene," said Minister of Aviation J.K. McAlpine. "Air New Zealand will get our country's and our airline's message to the world in the most direct and compelling way. It says what it means and it means what it says. It is a name which well suits the country's chosen instrument of international aviation."

Chairman Andrew McKee said the change would make each of the company's aircraft a "flying advertisement for New Zealand's tourist industry and sales promotion efforts abroad". The new company name would remind people of the destination from which it flew and in which it needed to arouse interest so those people would fly there.

"Air New Zealand is part of the big export business of tourism," says retired executive Richard Gates. "We sell and collect revenue overseas but bring the customers here to experience it. The company name helps with that."

In the years since the change, especially around the turn of the millennium, the New Zealand national brand itself has grown stronger internationally, so that carrier and destination are good for each other's business.

The logistics of the changeover are described by I.A. Thomson in his thesis, *A History of TEAL: The Origins of Air New Zealand as an International Airline*: "The change of name came into effect at midnight, 31 March 1965, when one of TEAL's Electras, *Atarua*, was nearing the end of an Auckland-Nadi service, so that a flight which had begun with a TEAL take-off was concluded with an Air New Zealand touchdown.

"The honour of making the first complete flight under the new banner went to the Electra *Aotearoa*, which left Sydney shortly after midnight on a trip to Auckland. Each aircraft was given the new company title as soon as possible, but in order to avoid any confusion which might have arisen from a sudden change, the name TEAL was retained in a subsidiary role for a transition period of about 12 months, and throughout this period the company's aircraft bore the new and old names."

Above Though TEAL became Air New Zealand in 1965, its flight designators remained "TE" until the 1980s, prompting some creative design by the airline.

The way they wore

The 1960s was a decade in which fashion was revolutionised – in the air as well as on land.

From 1961, TEAL's hostesses became the first in the world to have a wardrobe designed by the Parisian House of Dior. The official description was: "White silk blouse and turquoise pure worsted Trico tine skirt. Cravat top of blouse displayed over the rounded, collarless neckline of jacket. Blouse and skirt banded together with wide belt giving top a blouson effect which looks like a one-piece dress. Topcoat with set-away collar to show cravat. Pillbox style hat." The uniforms were made by local Christian Dior representatives El-Jay New Zealand. They were described as tailored, elegant and timeless with a new level of sophistication and style.

Right The Dior uniform accompanied with the classic 1960s accessory – the duffle bag.

updated Dior hostess'
uniform and the
stewards' uniforms
which came into
service on the DC-8.

crew meets kiwi, and
both are magnificent
in their plumage. This
kiwi was donated to
San Diego Zoo.

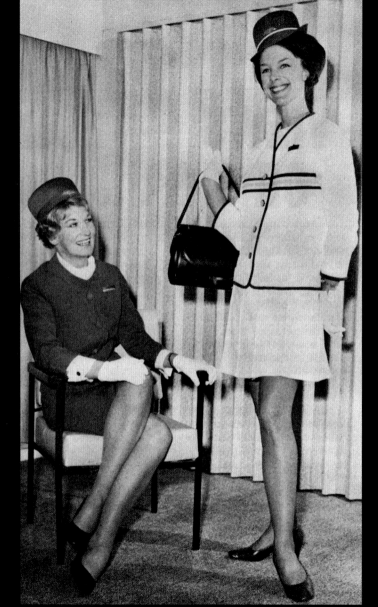

In 1965 NAC introduced the Golden Cloud uniform with its "Colman's mustard pot" hats under which, allegedly, curlers were frequently worn. Jewellery, earrings and nail varnish were forbidden accessories. In 1969, Jennifer Mann, an Air New Zealand Auckland Airport Traffic staff member designed a new uniform for the front-line ground staff. The uniform was a more suitable weight for the work they had to do. A white crimplene two-piece was introduced for traffic receptionists in 1969 and booking officers in 1970.

From 1969 to 1973, a new look was also introduced for flight hostesses – without abandoning their tailored Dior-designed outfits, which had lost none of their contemporary feel or appeal. In flight, hostesses changed to kaftans in four colours – turquoise, watermelon pink, lilac and strawberry – with a stylised hibiscus motif on the sleeves. The caftan was the major item in the introduction of a hibiscus theme aboard DC-8 and Electra aircraft, emphasising the South Pacific market which the airline served. This was known as the lollipop or jelly-bean style and was said to reflect "the age of liberalisation".

Left A staff member should know what staff need in a uniform, and Jennifer Mann's new design (right) was a hit with her colleagues. Jenny Mann is shown in the earlier Dior-designed uniform.

Left: The hat that became known as the "mustard pot".

Above The famous kaftan of the 1960s, worn by hostesses during the flight.

The jet set

Below An innovative 44-louvre tri-vision billboard on Wilshire Boulevard in Los Angeles advertised the new DC-8 service to and from the US.

Right The DC-8's arrival at Christchurch Airport drew a crowd of eager planespotters out to see the aircraft for themselves.

The sight of a propellor is a rare one these days, but for much of Air New Zealand's early history that's how aircraft were powered. With the arrival of the jet engine, faster planes and shorter flights changed everything.

The jet era began for TEAL when it took delivery of its first Electra – a jet-prop (combined jet and propeller technology) aircraft in November 1959. In the decade that followed, TEAL became a fully fledged participant in the jet era when it began to add DC-8 jets to the fleet.

The Electras were more than adequate craft – in 1963 one made a record crossing of the Tasman in two hours and 52 minutes – but they were not sufficient to meet the company's ambitious plans for long-term growth.

Politics bedevilled the search for an aircraft that would allow the company not only to fly more people further but also, in particular, to position itself in the travel market as the international carrier for the Pacific Rim.

The search for a bigger, faster jet was undertaken around the time that the question of Britain's entry into the European Common Market was in the air. Fearing such a move would lead to restrictions on imports from New Zealand, politicians put pressure on the airline to buy a British plane to keep that country on side. However, as far as TEAL was concerned, the American McDonnell Douglas DC-8 was the superior choice and their wishes would prevail in the end.

"The DC-8 was an absolutely massive step up in terms of technology," says a former executive. "It gave Air New Zealand the ability to expand dramatically. It meant we could fly to the US, Singapore, Hong Kong and pretty well anywhere. It achieved the company's goal of transforming itself from a small trans-Tasman airline that flew to Australia and some Pacific islands into an international airline."

Such an aircraft also demanded better facilities. Air New Zealand was only able to enter the jet age because some years previously a commitment had been made to build a new international airport for Auckland at Mangere.

Above The DC-8 was a huge advance on the technology that had preceded it but presented many challenges for crew as they adjusted to it.

Right First-class inflight service could now equal anything to be found on the ground.

Far right Comfortable economy seating in the DC-8.

"I will leave this earth for other places." If I can't then the Wright Brothers will. (with apologies to Leonardo da Vinci: circa. 1452-1519)

Thanks Leo. For your foresight, forsooth, we of AIR NEW ZEALAND salute you. And for that matter, we salute Orville and Wilbur, too.

We pay homage to all intrepid birdmen in this world of ours, who, through their work, courage and good old-fashioned know-how, have developed the heavier-than-air flying machine from a "mechanical contraption" to the 10 mile per minute Douglas DC-8 Jetliner, on which today, it is our pleasure to have

Mr. F. Maurice Clarke

as a distinguished passenger.

Gone, Leo, are the months of sitting astride a floating log at the mercy of tide and wind to visit sick relatives or enjoy annual leave. Today, Leo, with the development of modern aviation and the AIR NEW ZEALAND DC-8 Five Star Jetliner in particular, one can travel from Point A to Point B in a few short hours and for that matter, from B to A, providing one has a return ticket. And so, Leo, Orville and Wilbur too, at 30,000 feet above this worried world of ours, I pen my signature to this document with the knowledge that our aforementioned distinguished guest will cherish and keep it as a fitting souvenir of his, or her, flight in an AIR NEW ZEALAND DC-8 Jetliner.

DATE **24/3/66.**

AIR NEW ZEALAND CAPTAIN
Intrepid Birdman, 20th Century Vintage

➤ AIR NEW ZEALAND ★ ★★THE FIVE STAR JETLINE

In the South Island, Christchurch's Harewood airport was upgraded to meet the new aircraft's extra demands.

Air New Zealand established a new jet base at Mangere with a hangar that could hold three DC-8s as well as workshops, stores, flight kitchen, training school, engine testing cell and offices. Most engineering facilities were also moved to Mangere from their historic base at Mechanics Bay.

NAC acquired jets later in the decade. It too had to argue the case with the government for buying American, with its sights set firmly on the Boeing 737, the aircraft that would become the world's most successful commercial jet. NAC's first 737 flight took place between Auckland and Wellington in October 1968.

This was a decade of rapid growth, made possible by the capability of the jets with their increased range and passenger capacity. Between 1963 and 1967, Air New Zealand doubled its staff, passenger numbers increased from 102,341 to 231,709, and the number of kilometres flown grew from 224 million to 636 million.

Along the way, the introduction of the DC-8s had unintended consequences for some personnel. Among first officers, many experienced flyers had not got around to acquiring the flight navigator's licence that was a pre-requisite for getting a command. Suddenly, many positions became available and promotions were there for the taking. Many first officers who had had the foresight to get their licence were able to leapfrog ahead of more senior colleagues.

The aircraft also presented other issues. The DC-8's higher landing speed, for instance, meant that cockpit procedures were effectively "sped up" for the pilots and their response time had to be adjusted accordingly. Shorter flight times affected inflight drinking and dining. There was less time for the leisurely service that had been the practice in the past – at the same time, the bigger jets also meant there were more passengers to be served.

At the end of the decade, now established as an international airline of the jet age, Air New Zealand was ready to grow again. It decided to acquire some of the wide-bodied jets that were now in production and ordered three DC-10s.

A spectacular air pageant featuring displays of formation flying was among the highlights of the official opening in January 1966.

International arrival

29–31 January 1966

The opening of Auckland International Airport, the country's biggest, on an old aero club site, allowed the national airline to plan for even more ambitious growth in years to come.

Top left Thousands thronged from all over New Zealand to see the most modern airport in the country. NAC was in buying mode and this BAC-111 was effectively a flying demo model.

Left Mangere's location was ideal for its purposes and has allowed considerable room for expansion. Parking was at a premium on the opening day.

Tag team

UNION AIRWAYS

NATIONAL AIRWAYS
HAMILTON
MRS. HORSLEY.
D 12995 WEIGHT lbs.

Ski South

Royal
Over-seas League
New Zealand
Members'
World Tour

PLANNED AND BOOKED THROUGH

NAC

NEW ZEALAND NATIONAL AIRWAYS CORPORATION

AIR NEW ZEALAND
FIJI OPEN
FJ ____
5 AUGUST

AIR NEW ZEALAND
FIJI OPEN
FJ ____
5 AUGUST

BRITISH ISLES RUGBY TEAM

travelling by

NAC

NEW ZEALAND'S NATIONAL AIRLINE

NAC

OPERATION PEGASUS

MOUNT COOK AIRLINES

Name : _____ Weight : _____ Flt. _____
ON ARRIVAL AT CONNECTING AIRFIELD WE
WILL **TRANSHIP** THIS BAG TO
NAC FOR CARRIAGE ON FLT. _____
TO **AUCKLAND**

MOUNT COOK AIRLINES
P.O. BOX 2086, CHRISTCHURCH

YOUR BAGGAGE WILL BE TRANSHIPPED
FOR CARRIAGE ON A CONNECTING NAC
FLIGHT TO AUCKLAND
UNLESS FURTHER LABELLED "AIRPORT
ONLY" IT WILL BE AVAILABLE AT THE
NAC AUCKLAND AIRCENTRE

MT COOK AIRLINES

AIR NEW ZEALAND

Serving Singapore*, Hong Kong, Australia,
New Zealand, Fiji, Samoa, New Caledonia,
Norfolk Island, Tahiti, Hawaii, Los Angeles.
*(From December 16)

PRINTED IN NEW ZEALAND

(104) **History: 1970–1979**
Milestones and other memorable moments from the decade.

(110) **The final touchdown**
Grounding of the last DC-3.

(112) **The pilots' plane**
The shortlived glory of the DC-10.

(114) **The computer revolution**
The arrival of Air New Zealand's first computer.

(116) **National treasures**
NAC's artful early advertising.

(122) **Two become one**
Air New Zealand merges with NAC.

(124) **Anything for a laugh**
Cartoons of the era.

(125) **Sea and sky**
Air New Zealand was a pioneer of long-haul over-water flying.

(126) **Plane clothes operatives**
Nina Ricci-designed uniforms are introduced.

(128) **Flight TE901**
The sightseeing flight over Mount Erebus that became the darkest time in Air New Zealand's history.

=1979

NAC began the decade by moving into new Wellington headquarters, in July 1970. Eight years later, it was no more, after merging with bigger brother Air New Zealand in 1978. It was a move that Chairman Sir Geoffrey Roberts later described as "the right thing, done at the wrong time, in the wrong way". In the long term the benefits would become apparent.

At the other end of the decade, a tragedy that touched the nation and was the darkest of days for Air New Zealand occurred when Antarctic sightseeing flight TE901 crashed on Mount Erebus, killing all 257 people on board.

The intervening years had seen numerous developments. The decade farewelled DC-3s and Electras, and saw the advent of the wide-bodied jet, in this airline's case the McDonnell Douglas DC-10, which further broadened possibilities for travel and tourism. Air New Zealand took delivery of its first DC-10 in 1973.

In the same year it also introduced the Koru logo, which became an inseparable part of its identity.

Reflecting the importance of its freight operations, the carrier opened a new air cargo terminal building at Mangere in 1971, which it needed to expand just a few years later. The company also opened a new Auckland head office in Air New Zealand House.

Computerisation arrived, with Air New Zealand an early adopter of technology as it became available. Ticketing, reservations and other aspects of the flight experience would be revolutionised – for the better. The decade also witnessed the first fully automated landing and the first refrigerated cargo container.

In a similar spirit of innovation, Air New Zealand came to an agreement with British Airways under which the former's crew flew Auckland to Los Angeles and the latter's crew from Los Angeles to London on the same Air New Zealand DC-10, simplifying arrangements for passengers and paving the way for a major new route.

Computerisation arrived, with Air New Zealand an early adopter of technology as it became available. Ticketing, reservations and other aspects of the flight experience would be revolutionised.

Top left Lollies on landing were all part of the service.

Top right The Koru, Air New Zealand's most enduring symbol, made its appearance.

Above NAC got new "Lollipop" uniforms and later merged with Air New Zealand.

Top far right Air New Zealand House was a new home that matched its occupier's stature.

Right The wide-bodied DC-10 joins the fleet.

1 October 1970
Unduplicated route mileage increases from 42,659 to 49,283 through establishment of routes between Nadi and Honolulu, and Nadi and Rarotonga.

May 1971
Opening of Air New Zealand's new air cargo terminal building at Mangere.

January 1972
Golden Age and Student Standby fares introduced on domestic flights.

August 1972
NAC acquires 100 percent shareholding in Safe Air Limited.

1 January 1973
Chairman Geoffrey Roberts receives a knighthood for services to aviation in the New Year Honours.

Above The cargo business reaches a point where a new purpose-built terminal is necessary.

Far left An early example of customer-focused fare structuring that has become a company trademark.

Left Commodore Geoffrey Roberts in air force uniform before he was knighted.

HISTORICAL EVENTS IN NEW ZEALAND
1970–79

1970
- Natural gas from Kapuni supplied to Auckland.
- United States Vice-President Spiro Agnew's visit to New Zealand is marked by rowdy anti-Vietnam War protests (left).
- "Cheryl Moana Marie" by John Rowles hits number one (right).

27 January 1973
Arrival of first DC-10 in Auckland.

1 April 1973
ANZAM computerised reservations system begins operating in Auckland.

July 1973
NAC carries its 20 millionth passenger.

4 December 1973
Inaugural DC-8 Coral Route service from Auckland to Tahiti via Nadi (Fiji), Pago Pago (American Samoa) and Rarotonga (Cook Islands).

January 1974
NAC begins selling its Viscount aircraft, which have been superseded by Boeing 737 jets.

1 April 1974
All Air New Zealand's daily services to North America now operated by DC-10 aircraft.

December 1974
Last commercial flight by an NAC DC-3.

21 January 1975
An Air New Zealand DC-10 makes its first fully automatic landing at Auckland International Airport.

3 November 1975
Air New Zealand's computer reservations system named TERRIER.

Top right A computerised reservations system sees the company at the forefront of adopting new technology.

Right The arrival of the first DC-10 at Rarotonga Airport creates a stir.

1971
- Tiwai Point aluminium smelter opens.
- Warkworth satellite station begins operation.
- The last regular steam-hauled train journey is made (left).

1972
- Equal Pay Act passed (right).
- Number of business computers reaches 200.
- Rowing eight win gold at Munich Olympic Games.

1973
- Naval frigate dispatched in protest against French nuclear testing in the Pacific (left).
- New Zealand's population reaches three million.
- Colour TV introduced.

1974
- Commonwealth Games held in Christchurch (right).
- Accident Compensation Corporation established.
- Economist W.B. Sutch charged with spying and acquitted.

15 February 1977

First day-trip to Antarctica. The DC-10 flight is commanded by Captain Ian Gemmell, with 235 passengers on board.

4 July 1977

Air New Zealand begins handling its own traffic and cargo functions at Los Angeles.

19 December 1977

Government announces proposal to merge Air New Zealand and NAC.

1 April 1978

Air New Zealand and NAC merge as Air New Zealand.

29 August 1978

In their final year as separate companies, Air New Zealand records a net profit of $5.5 million, and NAC a net profit of $2.9 million.

Top right Food services continued to be developed throughout the decade.

Right The majestic barren landscape of Antarctica had always fascinated its near neighbours in New Zealand.

8 May 1979

Boeing 737 equipped with a galley to serve hot meals on Samoa and Fiji services.

17 February 1979

Fokker Friendship, ZK-NFC, crashes in Manukau Harbour on approach to Auckland International Airport, killing Captain Tony Circuitt and ground engineer John Forbes.

the Antarctic experience

air new zealand

1975
- Lynne Cox becomes the first woman to swim across Cook Strait (right).
- The Waitangi Tribunal is established.
- Second TV channel starts broadcasting.

- Whina Cooper leads a hikoi to Parliament seeking land rights (left).
- Daylight saving introduced.

1976
- New Zealand's national day, 6 February, renamed Waitangi Day.
- Matrimonial Property Act passed.

7 June 1979

All DC-10s worldwide grounded following United States Federal Aviation Administration withdrawal of DC-10 type certification.

14 July 1979

DC-10 grounding order lifted, allowing flights to the US to resume.

18 July 1979

Air New Zealand records consolidated profit of $8 million after first year of merger.

18 September 1979

New flight kitchen opened at Auckland, covering 2600sq m. It is capable of producing more than one million meals a year.

28 November 1979

DC-10, ZK-NZP, crashes on Mount Erebus in Antarctica while on a sightseeing flight. All 257 people on board are killed, including 24 crew and staff.

Left The recovery team endured difficult conditions at the crash site of TE901.

Bottom left Part of the upper fuselage showing door and cabin windows.

Below A near traffic jam of DC-10s when the aircraft are grounded around the world.

1977
- National Superannuation scheme begins.
- The 200 nautical mile (370km) exclusive economic zone is established.

- Introduction of metric system of weights and measures.
- The first New Zealand McDonald's opens in Porirua.

- Carless days introduced to reduce petrol consumption.

1978
- *Victory Over Death 2* by Colin McCahon (right) is presented to the National Gallery of Australia.

1979
- Ivan Mauger wins record sixth world speedway title (left).

The final touchdown

December 1974

After 27 years, the DC-3, which had kept so many New Zealanders connected, finally gave way to the jet age for good in 1974. The last scheduled flight on one of the original aeroplanes was between Christchurch and Timaru.

Left NAC DC-8s ZK-AOD *Papango* and ZK-AOH *Pateke* being readied for flight in December 1950.

Right A smooth landing for a DC-3 in 1974, its last year of service.

The pilots' plane

Left The first DC-10 ZK-NZL being welcomed at Christchurch Airport on 15 February 1973.

Below Roomy first-class facilities made the DC-10 a favourite with passengers.

Bottom Inflight service on the DC-10.

The DC-10 was not just an engineering and aviation triumph, it marked a step up in passenger comfort and allowed for new levels of inflight service, but it was also dogged by misfortune…

Ask a pilot who has been around for a while to name their favourite aircraft and odds are they will nominate the DC-10.

A new era of "jumbo" jets dawned when Pan Am launched its Boeing 747 services in 1970. Although an attractive option, the 747 was too big for Air New Zealand's needs, and an order was placed for three DC-10s on 15 September 1970.

"It was the perfect aeroplane for a pilot," says one who flew the DC-10. "It handled beautifully. It was the culmination of a long series of developments. From the point of view of technical capability, etc, the Lockheed Electra had been miles ahead of the DC-6. Then we got the DC-8 and it was three steps back. It was very basic. Then the DC-10 came along, and it was beautiful."

The DC-10 was a supremely comfortable plane for crew and passengers. In the first-class cabin there was enough space for a steward to wheel a joint of beef out on a trolley and carve it to the passenger's liking.

"Compared to the 747, the DC-10 was far advanced in its cockpit management system," says a former executive. "It was a great leap forward in terms of the number of passengers carried and comfort levels. It also gave Air New Zealand the ability to expand further. Thanks to it, the airline

entered a period when major strategic decisions were made in terms of how we marketed and sold our product. When we got rid of them and bought the first 747s, it was almost a step back."

But the DC-10 gained a reputation as an unlucky aircraft, not least because of the tragedy on Mount Erebus but also because of other accidents around the world.

After an accident on take-off at Chicago, when an engine detached, the US Federal Aviation Administration withdrew its operating certificate – effectively grounding DC-10s around the world with potentially disastrous financial consequences for the airlines concerned.

"It put Air New Zealand into crisis," says the former executive. "Virtually our whole fleet were DC-10s. We only had a couple of DC-8s so that created huge difficulties. We operated our DC-8s and leased in some 747s from Pan Am and Qantas. But we also lost a lot of passengers, giving them away to other airlines. So the financial drain on us was huge."

Eventually the decision was made to change the fleet from DC-10s to 747s.

"It was such a sad thing the DC-10 finished when it did," says the former pilot. "It still had plenty of capability left."

Top left Computer equipment at Newton Data Centre.

Far left The domestic traffic section at Auckland Airport monitored all internal aircraft movements within New Zealand.

Above Office workers at Air New Zealand House, 1 Queen Street.

Left The NAC Domestic Reservations System showing the wall status boards managed manually, 1974.

The computer revolution

The first computers to be used in the airline industry were giant, noisy machines that nevertheless made previously cumbersome and time-consuming processes such as reservations and bookings more efficient.

Computerisation revolutionised all businesses but none more so than air travel. In the case of Air New Zealand, the transformation began in the 1970s. At the start of the decade, NAC got DORAC – Development of Reservations and Communications – a semi-automated system, and the first of a long list of clunky acronyms that would appear over the years.

Before computers, bookings and reservations were complex and cumbersome operations involving manual status boards, cards, many pieces of paper, teleprinters and the potential for much frustration and writer's cramp.

The company was an early adopter of new technology and has remained in the vanguard.

"In the early days," remembers a former executive, "when the internet hadn't been thought of and computerisation was starting to come into the airline business, we thought it was revolutionary. Air New Zealand were leaders in information technology. We introduced computerised reservations systems, computerised ticketing. There were no businesses running as much through computers."

They were bold moves. As James S. Martin notes in *The Way It Used to Be*, an unpublished history of aspects of technology at the airline, at "the start of automation, all this new technology was high cost. It needs to be noted that in these early years all computer equipment outside of the USA was expensive."

Those early machines seem basic today. Both terminals and printers had noisy cooling fans, and the "green screens" were only able to access the mainframe – no word processing and certainly no internet access.

But the shift to computers was vital to Air New Zealand's success as it sought to become a fully fledged international airline: suddenly, the tyranny of distance seemed that much smaller.

Go there by **NAC**

Pahutu Geyser, Rotorua

NEW ZEALAND

be fashionable... fly **NAC** jet prop

ZK-BRG

NEW ZEALAND NATIONAL AIRWAYS CORPORATION

NEW ZEALAND NATIONAL AIRWAYS CORPORATION

BREATHTAKING BEAUTY...
JET PROP TRAVEL...
NO EXTRA COST

FLY IN THE STILL EVENING AIR WITH **NAC**

Your National Airline

NEW ZEALAND NATIONAL AIRWAYS CORPORATION

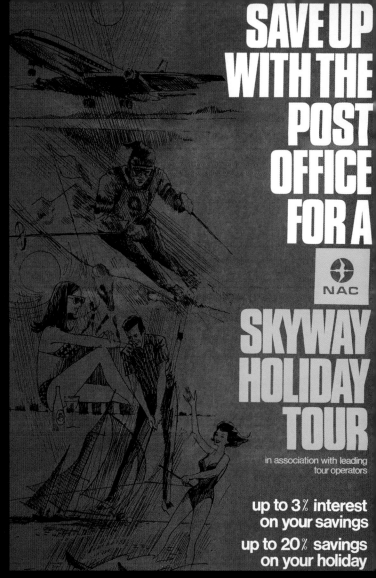

SAVE UP WITH THE POST OFFICE FOR A

NAC

SKYWAY HOLIDAY TOUR

in association with leading
tour operators

up to 3% interest
on your savings

up to 20% savings
on your holiday

NAC's posters beckoned travellers to New Zealand with promises that ranged from the breathtaking beauty of the destination to the savings that could be made on their bookings.

NAC AIR ATLAS

McKINLEY

travel in style with **NAC**
NEW ZEALAND'S NATIONAL AIRLINE

SAVE TIME...

USE THE POST OFFICE
AIR PARCEL
SERVICE

Above and top right There was more than one side to the Friendship – as a national icon and a stylish accessory.

Right The Vickers Viscount didn't just carry passengers, it could take care of all manner of parcels too.

whichever
way you want
to travel
book through
NAC
WORLD-WIDE
TRAVEL
SERVICE

Air, land and sea bookings
throughout the world.

Economy Tours, Cruises
and Group Travel.

Expert travel planning and
advisory service.

Prompt attention, quick
confirmation.

NEW ZEALAND NATIONAL AIRWAYS CORPORATION

Far left An NAC route
map shows a playful
display of Aotearoa's
offerings.

Left and above Airline
advertising came in
many forms, from
posters to brochures
and coasters.

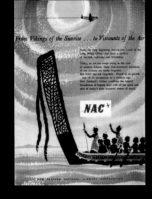

"Let me brief you on your flight"

WHERE IN THE WORLD ARE YOU GOING?

WORLD-WIDE TRAVEL SERVICE NAC

NEW ZEALAND NATIONAL AIRWAYS CORPORATION

Notornis Flies — on N.A.C. wings!

TO THE HOUSEHOLDER   POSTAGE PAID

NAC WORLD-WIDE TRAVEL SERVICE

Look at it from any angle...

NAC WORLD-WIDE TRAVEL SERVICE

FREE

SPECIAL SOUTH ISLAND HOLIDAY PACK

FLY SOUTH FOR A CHANGE

NAC
NEW ZEALAND'S NATIONAL AIRLINE

This page NAC found its way into New Zealanders' hearts (and letterboxes), appealing to cultural connections and the excitement of air travel

1970–1979

The nation's top marching girls' brigade starred in a successful NAC advertising promotion for print and television filmed in front of a Boeing 737 on the tarmac at Christchurch Airport.

This page NAC crew and TEAL ground staff at Rongatai Airport.

Opposite A colour change for some Air New Zealand aircraft as the airline absorbs NAC.

Two become one

For a small country, maintaining two Government-owned airlines with all the duplication and unnecessary expense that involved could not go on forever.

"It was the right thing, done at the wrong time, in the wrong way." That's how retired Air New Zealand chairman Sir Geoffrey Roberts summed up the merger of the national carrier NAC and the international airline in 1978.

For numerous logistical reasons the merger made good sense. One, cited by Neil Rennie in *Conquering Isolation*, was driven by changes in technology and associated increases in demand. This highlighted the need for a aircraft that could be used on domestic routes in peak times but also pressed into service to cross the Tasman when demand spiked on that route. It made sense for such a plane to be flown by one airline.

Other factors which made the merger more a necessity than a possibility were increased costs and growing pressure from international competitors across its routes.

Significantly, Qantas was showing signs of seeking an alliance with NAC and NAC was looking to return to flying some of the Pacific routes that it had given up years before; both measures put pressure on Air New Zealand. The logical solution to such pressure was a merger.

It was announced in September 1977 that the Ministry of Transport would undertake a study into the possibility of joining the two airlines together. In December, Prime Minister Robert Muldoon, who no one doubted called the shots, got right to the point and announced that the merger would take place – the following April.

Personnel from both airlines had hardly had time to get used to the news of the merger before it was a done deal. The speed with which it was made to happen led to problems whose fallout lingered for years. Morale plummeted, with many of the NAC staff feeling they had been involved in a takeover rather than a merger.

NAC's chief executive and general manager Doug Patterson found it particularly difficult. There had been behind-closed-doors negotiations and delays in the lead-up to the merger to which he had not been privy. However he took on a position as director of the merged Air New Zealand, partly, at least, to oversee the interests of his former staff.

The financial benefits of the merger did not filter through for some time. Air New Zealand had operating losses from 1980 to 1983, although asset sales in 1981 and 1982 enabled it to show a profit in those years.

It wasn't until the company started losing significant amounts of money that the government allowed its management to take the radical but necessary steps that were needed to restore it to profit.

In the long run, the merger can be seen as inevitable and practical. On the positive side, NAC had had a monopoly on air travel within New Zealand (part of its attraction for Qantas), and that monopoly benefited Air New Zealand when the merger took place. It gave Air New Zealand a foothold in the domestic market going overseas because local travellers heading to an international airport to go abroad would tend to stay with the same airline when they left the country. It also made it a bigger company, with a financial critical mass that enabled it to compete more aggressively with overseas airlines, such as Qantas, Continental, and Air Pacific, with which it went head to head on some routes.

NAC's only competition for people wanting to get from one part of New Zealand to another had been road and rail transport. Air New Zealand's competition was those other airlines with the same rights to fly to destinations and access to the same markets.

But there was little time to enjoy the competitive advantages of the merger, because before long the Lange Labour Government opened up the domestic market and Australia's Ansett was allowed to fly New Zealand domestic routes. It had been envisaged that Air New Zealand would gain reciprocal rights and be allowed to fly domestically within Australia, but somehow that never eventuated.

Ultimately, Ansett would create considerably more complications for Air New Zealand than a spat over flying within Australia.

Tuesday afternoon from Auckland.

Tuesday night from Auckland.

Wednesday morning from Invercargill.

Wednesday from Napier.

Thursday from Kaitaia.

You might not even think of yourself as a group...!
but fly this way and you can save 10% or more.

It's simple. If ten or more of you are travelling to the same destination within fourteen days, Air New Zealand Domestic Services will give you a Group Travel discount of 10%. Or more.

For full details ask for Your Airline's Group Travel brochure at your Air New Zealand booking office or Travel Agent.

Anything for a laugh

This page The airline used bold, humorous cartoons to promote its regional services.

Sea and sky

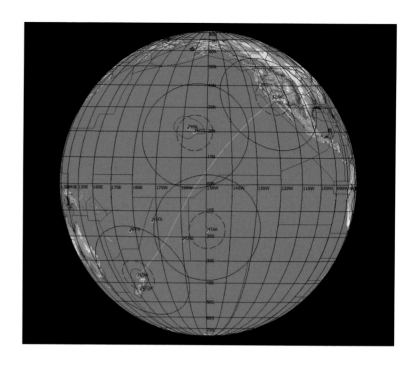

Flying long haul over oceans has always been part and parcel of Air New Zealand's operations. Now, the latest technology allows the airline to fly even further.

Because of New Zealand's unique location, surrounded by vast oceans, the ability to fly long distances safely over water has always placed unique demands on the airline. The move toward more economical twin-engine aircraft drove the development of a device to operate twins over water.

Today's aircraft can fly further from land for longer than ever before, making long-distance travel more comfortable and convenient than ever by allowing more straightforward routes and fewer stopovers.

Since 1953, safety regulations have limited how far a commercial twin-engine aircraft can fly from possible landing space. In the USA, early two-piston engine commercial aircraft were required to remain no further than 60 minutes from a suitable airport if traveling at the single-engine speed.

The International Civil Aviation Organisation (ICAO) allowed aircraft to fly as far as 90 minutes from a suitable airport at the twin-engine speed.

In February 1978, Air New Zealand was one of the first carriers to take advantage of the ICAO rule and twin-engine aircraft efficiencies when it began a Boeing 737-200 service from Auckland to Samoa. Although such pioneering might have looked risky, even in 1978 jet engines were at least 100 times more reliable than the early piston engines whose performance had led to the 60-minute rule.

The introduction of the B767-200ER in September 1985, using the new Extended Operations (ETOPS) requirements, saw the use of twin-engine aircraft over water expand rapidly.

ETOPS was based on a "preclude and protect philosophy". Aircraft are designed with more systems redundancy, to protect them from the consequence of failure, while higher reliability requirements preclude the chances of those failures occuring in the first place. This ushered in a new era with more demanding engine and aircraft system-reliability requirements, better maintenance procedures and enhanced flight-crew procedures. In the 30-plus years of its existence, ETOPS has driven the entire aviation system to achieve ever-higher levels of engine and airframe reliability.

Air New Zealand has continued to innovate and lead the world in twin-engine over-water operations. On December 7 1989 the carrier became the first to fly up to 180 minutes from a suitable airfield when it launched its Boeing 767 service between Honolulu and Los Angeles. And it didn't stop there.

On 3 December 2011 Air New Zealand became the first carrier to be approved to operate Boeing 777-300 aircraft up to 240 minutes from diversion airfields. Now, under the name Extended Diversion Time Operations (EDTO) the ability of twin-engine aircraft to fly anywhere is slowly coming to fruition, with Air New Zealand at the forefront of the evolution.

Air New Zealand is by far the largest Airbus A320 EDTO operator, accounting for around 80 percent of all EDTO flights. Overall Air New Zealand has more than 36 years and 2.2 million hours of ETOPS/EDTO experience. The B767 fleet alone has flown an impressive 1.1 million EDTO hours, the A320 fleet 450,000 hours and the B777 fleet 375,000 hours. Air New Zealand leads the EDTO world, a capability that is vital given the country is 1600km from its closest neighbour.

Plane clothes operatives

In 1976, a uniform for international crew was designed by the Parisian fashion house Nina Ricci and first presented to the public on television's *Town Cryer*. This debut was followed by a week of parades in Auckland, Dunedin, Wellington and Christchurch. Then it was across the Tasman for a week of promotions in Melbourne, Brisbane and Sydney that included parades and attracted radio, TV and newspaper coverage.

"More than 12,000 items, including shoes, handbags, hats and ties are needed for the complete changeover," reported the inhouse *Enzedair* before going on to reveal that "printed slub Terylene polyester fabric for the hostess's skirts and tops was specially spun in England to meet the... hard-wearing requirements".

It was described as featuring "a geometric border print in toning shades of blue and teal with white for use in a long skirt and top to wear on the dinner flights. A similar pleated short skirt and two shirts… are in the same fabric. The linen-look wool and synthetic fabric for the dress uniform was made in New Zealand and all females' garments mixed and matched elegantly."

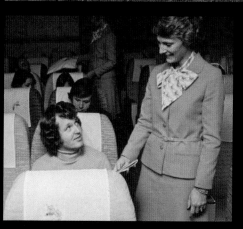

Flight TE901

Below One of the Disaster Victim Identification (DVI) team members at the crash site.

Bottom The battered tail of the ill-fated DC-10.

Opposite An aerial shot of the Mt Erebus crash site.

1970—1979

It was the darkest day in Air New Zealand's history and one of the darkest for the whole country. What started out as a thrilling sightseeing flight ended in a tragedy whose impact is still felt today.

On 28 November 1979, Air New Zealand Flight TE901, a DC-10 carrying passengers on a sightseeing trip to Antarctica, crashed into Mount Erebus, killing all 257 people on board.

Air New Zealand had been flying people to the southern continent for two years. The trips left Christchurch early in the morning, flew to and around parts of Antarctica and came back the same day. A flight over the mysterious icy landscape, otherwise inaccessible to all but the hardiest travellers, was one of the world's great sightseeing experiences and the trips had been popular from their inception.

Sir Edmund Hillary's former climbing companion Peter Mulgrew was a guide on board that day, having taken the place of Sir Ed, who was scheduled but unavailable.

The attempt to determine the factors responsible for the incident led to protracted and acrimonious court cases over several years, reaching as far as the Privy Council in London.

Notwithstanding any conclusion reached in that forum and others, along with numerous books, documentaries and other accounts, the argument over the ultimate cause for the disaster continues to this day.

What is beyond doubt is that the tragedy affected all New Zealand, not just Air New Zealand. In this small country it seems everybody at least knew someone who lost someone dear to them on the mountain.

Those who died are remembered in the hearts of those close to them and by several memorials, including a stainless-steel cross erected on Mount Erebus near the crash site in 1987. In October 2009, a memorial sculpture called "Momentum" was unveiled at a ceremony outside Air New Zealand headquarters, at which former CEO Rob Fyfe apologised to the families of the victims. Among many other memorials around the country is a garden at Auckland Airport that was planted to commemorate the crew who died.

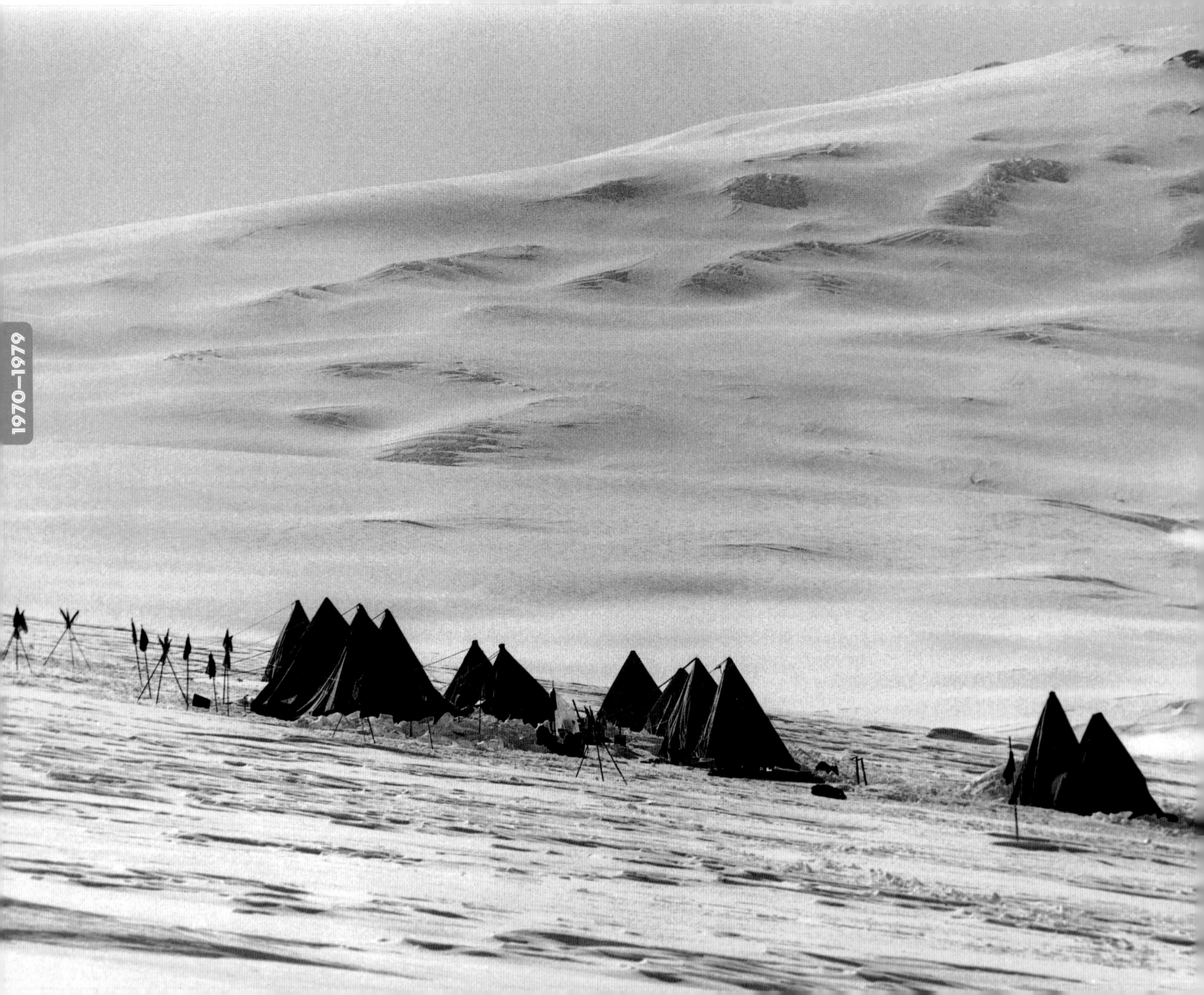

Left The recovery team campsite.

Right The last effort of the crash-site recovery team was to install a memorial cross, which was hand built by New Zealanders at Scott Base, and was used at the memorial service held there. The cross was flown to the site by helicopter. It was replaced in 1986 with a stainless-steel cross.

(134) **History: 1980–1989**
Milestones and other memorable moments from the decade.

(140) **Enter the jumbo**
How one aircraft fuelled an airline's expansion and changed how we fly.

(144) **A change in the air**
A radical rethink for uniforms.

(146) **London calling**
The opening up of a direct flight to London was a project that was years in the making.

(150) **Home comforts**
The Koru Lounge set new standards in service.

(152) **Drama at Nadi**
Sharp wits and a whisky bottle save the day.

(153) **The scenic route**
Mount Cook Airlines, Air Nelson and Eagle Air.

(154) **Pride and joy**
Celebrating the arrival of the Boeing 767.

(155) **Koru Care begins**
Staff get together to provide disadvantaged kids with experiences to remember.

(156) **Private life**
Sold! But not for very long.

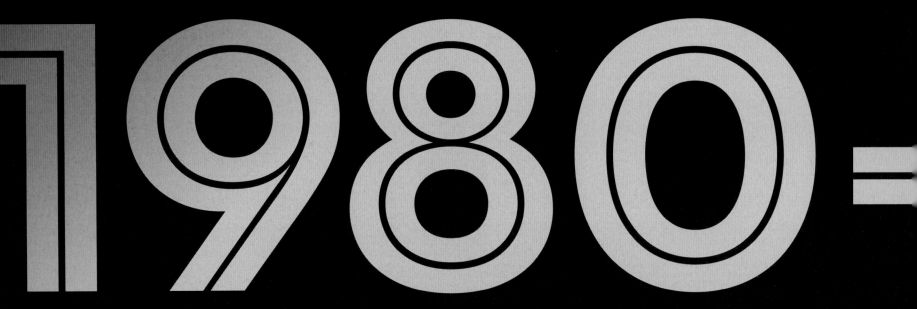

1980–

=1989

The decision was taken to sell the fleet of DC-10s and replace them with Boeing 747s. Five were ordered, signalling a fresh start for the airline.

Air New Zealand earned the right to fly to London in 1982. Not only did this become a very successful and profitable route, it gave the company a toehold in Europe, and its "Ritz of the skies" campaign established a reputation for creative promotions that would be developed over the decades. The 1980s also saw the arrival of the first Boeing 767s and Boeing 737-200 Advanced.

More routes were developed following a 1980 agreement giving rights to US destinations. And the business was developed further when the company entered into a joint venture to build the Sheraton Hotel (now the Langham) in Auckland.

On the inbound front, 1983 was the first year in which New Zealand hosted more than 500,000 visitors. In this year, too, Koru Care, a crew-initiated charity for special-needs and underprivileged children, was launched. And the first of Air New Zealand's Koru Lounges, members-only facilities, were opened in Auckland and Wellington in 1986.

Discounted "Thrifty Fares" for domestic destinations were introduced; innovative fare pricing would be another hallmark of Air New Zealand's business in years to come as it conceived new ways to fill unsold seats and maximise its returns. The later years of the decade saw some record profits following some difficult financial patches.

In 1987, a hijacking attempt on a Boeing 747 refuelling at Nadi Airport was foiled by Flight Engineer Graeme Walsh, who overpowered the armed hijacker with a well-aimed bottle of whisky.

A deregulation-minded, free market-oriented government – and a transport minister who was determined that industrial action by crew that had caused widespread disruption would not be repeated – decided to privatise the company at the end of the decade. There followed a complex series of trades whose final consequences would not be played out until years later.

The company's "Ritz of the skies" campaign established a reputation for creative promotions that would be developed over the decades. The 1980s also saw the arrival of the first Boeing 767s.

LONDON
Go all the way with Air New Zealand

Top The right to fly direct to London was a huge step forward for the airline.

Top right Air New Zealand's first 747 was unveiled, May 1981.

Right The London office opened in New Zealand House in the Haymarket, in December 1983.

12 June 1980
Agreement to purchase five Boeing 747-200s at an estimated cost of $335 million.

27 August 1980
Annual report for 1979-80 records loss on trading operations of $15.4 million, due mainly to increased costs and the DC-10 grounding.

25 November 1980
Bilateral agreement with the United States gives Air New Zealand the opportunity to fly to additional US destinations and points beyond.

4 March 1981
1200 Air New Zealand engineers end the two-week strike that almost brought the airline to a standstill.

27 March 1981
First DC-10 service to Tokyo – one week earlier than planned.

27 April 1981
Commission of Inquiry into the Mount Erebus tragedy released.

21 May 1981
Air New Zealand files statement of claim in High Court seeking review of certain allegations and findings made by Mr Justice Mahon in his report on Erebus.

29 May 1981
The first of five B747s arrives.

1 September 1981
Company announces net loss of $30.8 million in 1980-81 financial year.

December 1981
Court of Appeal determines that the findings by the Royal Commission into the Erebus disaster exceeded its terms of reference and violated natural justice. Order of costs against the company is quashed.

15 September 1982
Company announces record $90 million operating loss.

H. 1

N. 2. Report of the Royal Commission
to inquire into
The Crash
on
MOUNT EREBUS, ANTARCTICA
of a
DC10 AIRCRAFT
operated by
AIR NEW ZEALAND LIMITED
1981

Presented to the House of Representatives by Command of His Excellency the Governor-General

BY AUTHORITY:
E. D. HASSELBERG, GOVERNMENT PRINTER, WELLINGTON, NEW ZEALAND—1981

Price $9.60

Above The official report into the Air New Zealand crash on Mount Erebus, Antarctica.

HISTORICAL EVENTS IN NEW ZEALAND
1980–89

1980
- Saturday trading partially legalised.
- The Soviet ambassador Vsevolod Sofinsky, is expelled for giving money to the pro-Soviet Socialist Unity Party.
- "I Got You" by Split Enz (right) goes to number one in New Zealand, Australia and Canada.

1981
- South African rugby team's tour of New Zealand brings widespread disruption (right and opposite left).
- First kohanga reo established.
- Allison Roe wins New York and Boston marathons.

6 December 1982

ZK-NQC Boeing 737 *Quick Change*, a new passenger/freighter aircraft, arrives in Christchurch from Seattle. This 10th Boeing 737 can change roles in one hour.

18 July 1983

Air New Zealand offers "Thrifty Fares" with reductions of 43 percent on selected evening flights between Auckland, Wellington and Christchurch.

3 August 1983

Operating loss for the 1982-83 financial year reported at $32.5 million. Through the sale of four DC-10 aircraft, company returns overall net profit of $33.6 million.

20 October 1983

Privy Council upholds Court of Appeal decision on findings of Royal Commission into the Erebus disaster.

29 November 1983

A first for New Zealand tourism – the 500,000th visitor in one year arrives.

5 December 1983

Air New Zealand increases its shareholding in The Mount Cook Group to 30 percent.

1 April 1984

First non-stop B747 flight from Auckland to Los Angeles as part of weekly one-stop service to London. Journey time of 24 hours is fastest from New Zealand to United Kingdom.

17 August 1984

Operating profit of $79 million against previous year loss of $32.5 million.

9 July 1985

Annual revenue exceeds $1 billion for the first time.

18 July 1985

Air New Zealand is given approval to purchase 77 percent share of The Mount Cook Group Ltd.

AIR NEW ZEALAND WILL SHOW YOU THAT ALL 747s ARE NOT CREATED EQUAL

TIMETABLE

MT. COOK AIRLINES
NEW ZEALAND
BY DC3 AIRCRAFT

TOURIST CO. LTD

TIMETABLE
PASSENGER FARES
FREIGHT RATES
INFORMATION
ROUTE MAP

EFFECTIVE
1st APRIL, 1966 to
20th DECEMBER, 1966

Cancels all previous timetables

Top right Mount Cook Airlines ski plane on the Tasman Glacier.

Right Promoting new first-class seating on the 747-200.

Far right Mount Cook timetable and fare guide. Air New Zealand increased its shareholding to 30 percent in 1983.

1982
- Queen of crime writers, Dame Ngaio Marsh (right) dies.
- First New Zealand football team to compete at FIFA World Cup.

1983
- Signing of CER agreement strengthens trans-Tasman trade ties.
- Visit of Prince Charles and Princess Diana (left). Prince William encounters the Buzzy Bee.

1984
- Auckland's population exceeds that of the South Island.
- Minister of Finance Roger Douglas begins deregulating the economy.

- A suitcase bomb explodes in Wellington's Trades Hall, killing caretaker Ernie Abbott (left).

1980–1989

10 September 1985
The first Boeing 767-219ER (ZK-NBA) delivered. The B767 was purchased to reintroduce Tasman services into Wellington.

21 January 1986
The first of six new Boeing 737-200 Advanced aircraft (ZK-NAT) makes its delivery flight.

1 July 1986
Government allows up to 50 percent foreign ownership of New Zealand domestic airlines.

24 November 1986
Air New Zealand Boeing 767 operates special charter Christchurch-Canberra for Pope John Paul II and entourage.

9 December 1986
Air New Zealand opens fully equipped Koru Lounges for domestic air travellers.

19 May 1987
Attempted hijacking of Air New Zealand Boeing 747 at Nadi airport thwarted when a member of the crew strikes the hijacker on the head with a whisky bottle.

7 October 1987
Australian government confirms prohibition on foreign carriers flying domestic routes and restricts foreign ownership of domestic airlines to 15 percent.

22 February 1988
The New Zealand Government allows Australian airline Ansett to buy 100 percent control of a New Zealand domestic airline.

June 1988
Air New Zealand achieves a net profit after tax of $70.4 million.

16 September 1988
Air New Zealand takes a 50 percent shareholding in regional carriers Eagle Air and Air Nelson.

Top Pope John Paul II presents Air New Zealand crew with a papal medal in recognition of services given by the company.

Above Australia's Ansett receives government approval to purchase 100 percent of a New Zealand domestic airline.

1985
- Greenpeace vessel *Rainbow Warrior* is bombed and sunk by French agents in Auckland harbour (right).
- New Zealand dollar floated.
- First EFTPOS cards issued.

- "Te Maori" exhibition opens in New York.
- *The Bone People* by Keri Hulme wins the Booker Prize.

1986
- Goods and Services Tax introduced.
- First visit to New Zealand by the Pope.
- "Slice of Heaven" by Dave Dobbyn (left) with Herbs hits number one.

1987
- Share prices plummet by 59 percent in four months.
- Maori Language Act is passed, making Maori an official language.

3 October 1988
Smoking banned on all domestic flights.

31 October 1988
Provincial routes serviced by Air New Zealand's Fokker F27 aircraft replaced by Eagle Air and Air Nelson aircraft.

20 December 1988
Government announces sale of Air New Zealand. Brierley Investments Ltd will take 65 percent with 30 percent to be onsold to the New Zealand public, staff and institutional investors. Qantas with 19.9 percent, Japan Airlines 7.5 percent, American Airlines 7.5 percent and a government "Kiwi" share make up the balance. This share has special powers to ensure that the majority shareholding is held by New Zealanders.

July 1989
Air New Zealand announces its annual revenue boosted to a record $1.7 billion.

29 October 1989
Under a joint service agreement between Air New Zealand and Qantas, 10 weekly Tasman flights will be code-shared – six to be operated by Qantas aircraft and crew, and four by Air New Zealand.

1 December 1989
Twentieth annual "Operation Santa" flight, taking special-needs and disadvantaged children for a one-hour festive Christmas flight around New Zealand.

Top The Beechcraft 1900D became a familar sight in smaller airports around the country.

Middle An Air Nelson Piper Pa-31 Navajo on the tarmac.

Bottom Eagle Air started as a flying academy and turned into a commuter airline, before being purchased by Air New Zealand.

- The New Zealand Nuclear Free Zone, Disarmament, and Arms Control Act becomes law.
- New Zealand wins Rugby World Cup (right).

- The State-Owned Enterprises Act marks a major overhaul of the public sector.
- Lotto goes on sale for the first time (right).

1988
- New Zealand Post closes 432 post offices.
- Fisheries quota package announced for Maori iwi.

1989
- Prime Minister David Lange suggests formal withdrawal from ANZUS.
- First annual balance of payments surplus since 1973.

- Sunday trading begins.
- TV3 begins broadcasting.
- *Holmes* show is launched on TV One.

The Boeing 747-200
revolutionised the way
Air New Zealand did
business in the 1980s.

1980–1989

Enter the jumbo

The arrival of its first fleet of Boeing 747s marked the beginning of a new era for the airline, fuelling expansion throughout the decade and beyond.

The Boeing 747 in its various versions is undoubtedly one of the most successful aircraft of all time, partly due to its sheer commercial appeal and the numbers sold – 1500 and counting in 2014 – but also for the way it embedded itself in the public consciousness. As the first of the wide-bodied, long-haul aircraft, with its distinctive "bumped" cockpit, it is for many people the epitome of the jet age, more than earning the title "jumbo jet".

The aircraft had been used by Air New Zealand some time before it actually purchased any. When the DC-10 fleet was grounded around the world in mid-1979, the airline chartered several 747s to move a backlog of passengers on its Auckland-Los Angeles route. Air New Zealand had had the opportunity to buy 747s when they were launched in 1970, but at that time the carrier had no need to acquire an aircraft with such a large capacity. Within a decade, many people had lost confidence in the DC-10 because of the number of incidents in which it had been involved around the world. Air New Zealand decided to divest itself of its fleet and replace it with 747s. By that time the airline, poised for expansion, did indeed need the capacity afforded by the Boeing aircraft.

It wasn't a decision made lightly or hastily. Former executive Richard Gates and a team spent a significant amount of time at Boeing headquarters in Seattle, considering the purchase.

"The 747s we got were well configured, nicely put together with good seats and generally a great thing," says Gates. "People don't realise that evaluating aircraft is quite complex – each aircraft has different capabilities and you have to apply them to your route structure. For example, we operate into airfields that are hot and high. We operate into ones that had different weather patterns, different runway lengths, etc. The aircraft has to be right for the conditions."

The airline acquired its first five 747s in 1981-82. After a period in the relative doldrums, it was an inspiring move. The first aircraft arrived in Auckland on 29 May 1981, and many greeting it had tears in their eyes because they felt they were witnesses to a great new beginning. In quick succession, and as other aircraft arrived, the 747 joined major routes – Sydney, Melbourne, Brisbane, Singapore, Nadi, Honolulu and Los Angeles. A landmark flight was the first non-stop journey from Auckland to Los Angeles and on to London, on 1 April 1984. At a flight-time of 24 hours, this was the fastest Auckland-London journey possible and also brought the number of 747 services to Los Angeles to 10 a week.

The increased capacity fed expansion through the 1980s. Initially, however, pilots hankered for the DC-10 and took some time to adjust. One described it as a "step into the dark ages". Another observer voiced a common opinion: "The 747 cockpit was basically analogue. The DC-10 was far more advanced in its cockpit management system, with more technology, and certainly a nicer aircraft to fly."

History has proven Air New Zealand's choice correct. The last DC-10 was produced in 1989. The 747 and its variants were still being produced in 2014, pointing the way ahead for air travel and the changing needs of travellers. In 1992, for instance, Air New Zealand's new Boeing 747-400 arrived on a non-stop 11,494km flight from Seattle. With capacity for 436 passengers, cruising at 900kph and with a range of 13,000km, the 747-400 allowed services to be increased to a variety of destinations, including four flights a week to London, two a week to Frankfurt and daily services to Melbourne.

With the introduction of the 777 fleet and Air New Zealand's changing needs, the 747 was gradually phased out, with the final flight from San Francisco in September 2014.

OUR PACIFIC CLASS PUTS YOU IN A CLASS OF YOUR OWN.

You've never experienced a business-class cabin like our exclusive Pacific Class.

It's reached by a gently sloping stairway that leads you to an upper-deck cabin.

You'll find 16 lambswool-clad seats, with some separated by a fold-down table.

An exclusive menu served by a personal cabin attendant.

Free, soft muff-type headphones.

And complimentary drinks served in the finest glassware.

Out of sight side-storage lockers accommodate all hand luggage, plus you have the privacy of your own toilets.

And all the peace you would expect in your own Pacific paradise.

You'll realise why we're the Pacific's Number One.

THE PACIFIC'S NUMBER ONE

DAILY TO THE USA

TARB Licence No: B192

Dailey/AP 936

🌀 **air new zealand**

WE PAID $8,000 EACH FOR OUR 1st CLASS CHAIRS. FORTUNATELY THEY WON'T COST YOU AS MUCH.

The chairs in the First Class Cabin of our new 747 Super B cost us around $8,000 each.

Designed and manufactured by Recaro in West Germany, these fully contoured chairs hydraulically recline a full 60 degrees without an uncomfortable bump or "step" effect.

This leaves your feet at the same level as your heart, medically the ideal position for complete body rest. And because there are only 16 staggered chairs in the cabin, you receive maximum privacy.

Needless to say, the cabin service and menu are what you would expect from Air New Zealand. No wonder we're the Pacific's Number One.

THE PACIFIC'S NUMBER ONE

DAILY TO THE USA

TARB Licence No: B192

Dailey/AP 932

🌀 **air new zealand**

Above Advertising Air New Zealand's new Pacific Class in the 747 "bubble".

Above right The 747's fully reclining First Class cabin seats were the forerunner to today's lie-flat beds.

Soaring high above the heavens

The arrival of the Boeing 747s with their spacious business and first-class cabins revolutionised travel for New Zealanders and quickly opened up new routes for the airline.

Right The wide-bodied "jumbo jet" soon became a family favourite with its roomy economy seats, which took some of the pain out of long-haul flights.

Right The new Isabel Harris uniform, with hat, coat and cabin bag, echoed the airline's brand colours.

Far right Poly-cotton overblouse and skirt with subtle Koru motif on squares of navy and teal and a white background.

international and domestic cabin crew to "pick up the vibes" of what she should pay attention to. She settled on teal as the main colour early in the process, saying the attendants were "lucky to have that as the corporate colour – being mid-range it suits all sorts of people". A new introduction in the Harris uniform was a blouse and skirt made from poly-cotton, featuring a "patterned print with a subtle Koru motif in random squares of navy and teal on a white background".

The collection had many combinations of the basic colours of teal and navy. The dress uniform in mid-teal featured a double-breasted jacket with brass buttons and epaulettes.

London calling

One of Air New Zealand's most significant and successful routes is the flight to London via Los Angeles. It took years of hard work to organise the rights and bring this long-held dream to fruition.

If the introduction of DC-8s had secured Air New Zealand's position as an international airline, the advent of the DC-10 with its greater capacity and reach enabled it to become a global force. However, this didn't happen overnight.

For some time Air New Zealand was an "offline carrier" between its home country and Great Britain. This meant that although it could sell flights to the other side of the world, it shared the route with another airline, in this case, British Airways. The two operated a joint flight, with British Airways chartering an aircraft from Air New Zealand at Los Angeles. An Air New Zealand plane would fly passengers to Los Angeles – at which point that plane would be taken over by the British Airways flight and cabin crews.

Such an arrangement is taken for granted today – the Global Star Alliance is a more elaborate version of the same principle. Back then it was innovative in the extreme – the sort of innovation for which Air New Zealand has always been known.

Obviously, the ideal was to be able to fly passengers on an Air New Zealand flight the whole way from Auckland to London. Links between New Zealand and Britain – while not what they were when the old country was regarded as "home" – were still strong, and the OE (overseas experience) market was burgeoning as young New Zealanders, not yet ready to settle down, set off to see the world. And Britain was by far and away the most favoured destination.

The first Auckland-London flight left Auckland on the evening of 25 August 1982 in a 747-200, flying via Papeete and Los Angeles. Everything possible was done to emphasise the sense of occasion for this momentous event. The flight was full so as to maximise impact when it landed. Dignitaries were on board, and British Airways, Air New Zealand's long-term partner, was a great help in making the event all it could be.

Richard Gates, who played a part in masterminding the Air New Zealand-London project recalls: "We didn't park on an air bridge, but parked out in the open for maximum visibility. The rain was coming down in torrents – a great London moment – but the minute we landed the sun came out. I had organised for

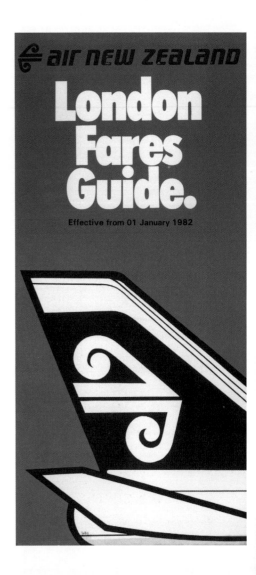

AIR NEW ZEALAND

London Fares Guide.

Effective from 01 January 1982

LONDON BRIDGE IS FOR SALE

⟋ air new zealand

LONDON BRIDGE FARES

$697
SPECIAL ONE WAY
LONDON

$1200
SPECIAL RETURN
LONDON

Air New Zealand brings you the $714.70* air fare to London and return

(Even less to other European cities)

ASK HERE!

AIR NEW ZEALAND

A GOOD DEAL GOING FOR YOU

*Economy class from Auckland, Wellington and Christchurch.
Effective from February 1 subject to Government approval.

with BOAC & QANTAS

"Look at London - isn't it just super!"

⟋ air new zealand

LONDON HOTEL SPECIAL

WESTMORLAND HOTEL **$37** PER NIGHT

Right in the heart of London
⟋ air new zealand

147

August 25th. Our first ever direct 747 to London. And already they're calling us 'the Ritz of the Skies.'

The Pacific's Number One

Travel writers can be sharp critics.

They've seen a lot of hotels and restaurants, a lot of airlines.

Seems we surprised a few.

The Breakfast Book preferred our breakfasts to most First Class hotels.

Travel Holiday Magazine voted Air New Zealand as Best Airline (two years running).

Was it our sheepskin covered seats? Our china plates and cups? Our wines? Our friendliness? Our style?

Your clients will decide.

Any Wednesday or Saturday, from August 25th* – they can be the sharpest critics of all. A great plus they'll like is having their baggage with them all the way.

"The Ritz of the skies."

That's what one travel writer called us. Even before we get there.

air new zealand

*Subject to Government approval.

DWME 3319A

The most pleasurable way to the U.K. Any day.

Point by point, your airline offers you the most pleasurable way to the U.K.

Take **frequency** as point one. Your airline can start you on your way to the U.K. **any** day you choose — 11 times each week to Los Angeles — 2 flights weekly to Hong Kong and Singapore.

Point two **stopover options**. Because your airline flies you to a choice of three gateway cities (Los Angeles, or Hong Kong, or Singapore) you have a wider choice straight away. Your airline connects you with British Airways flights to London (or the airline of your choice), giving you the chance to fly West one way, East the other. Going or coming, the choice is yours.

Which brings us to point three, **aircraft type**. Your airline operates the famous DC-10 — relaxed, spacious, yet with an intimate atmosphere you'll appreciate.

Point four is **in-flight service**. And it's the main reason your airline is so highly praised by overseas travellers. Fine wines, fine foods, the friendly cabin crew — these personal touches have made Air New Zealand famous.

So, on your trip to the U.K., remember Air New Zealand. Point by point, the most pleasurable way to the U.K.!

Make it your day with your airline, soon.

air new zealand

London 13 times weekly
(And what that means to you.)

It means you can make your U.K. travel plans to suit **your** needs . . . not those of a limited airline schedule. Air New Zealand flies you direct to Los Angeles. Or Singapore. Or Hong Kong. And from any of these three gateway cities we can make all the arrangements for your onward travel on British Airways, or the airline of your choice.

If you want to travel to the U.K. through the USA, Air New Zealand can get you to **London 9 times a week via Los Angeles.** Or if the Orient way is your choice, our wide-bodied DC-10s fly nonstop to **Singapore** twice each week. And we also have twice weekly flights to **Hong Kong.**

Your kind of fare
You can get our special one-way Auckland/London Fare for just **$637.** Or the Excursion Fare round-trip for just **$1118.** Or you may prefer to travel on the normal First Class or Economy Fares which offer many advantages. The point is, it's the way you want it.

Your kind of stopovers
If you'd like to see a little of Los Angeles, or Singapore, or Hong Kong, Air New Zealand has some sensational low budget stopover options. Just ask, and we'll make all the arrangements.

Buy now with London Shoppe
You can purchase your London or European tours and accommodation in advance here in New Zealand. It's so much more convenient to have everything taken care of. And such a saving too, with London Shoppe Tours. Get your copy of the colourful London Shoppe brochure now.

For London the way you want it, see your travel agent or Air New Zealand.

a welcome from a huge Maori concert party made up of members from local London Maori clubs. And we had hostesses in uniform from every airline that flew in there, holding up welcome signs."

There was a full panoply of events and advertising to launch the service as well. "We won a national marketing award in London for our advertising, which made sure that from day one the name of Air New Zealand was in the UK in a big way. We had a great stroke of luck in that our agency was Saatchi & Saatchi, who were not then as famous as they later became but were definitely daring and innovative.

"We had taken part in a newspaper survey on airlines and what they provided. You had to fill in a form saying what you were provided with in first class, business and economy and tick a box beside each thing. We just ticked every box and stuck it in. And we won. It was published in *The Times* and the article said, 'This airline must be the Ritz of the skies.' So that's the line we used to promote the airline. It was a bit naughty but we were certainly close to having everything in those boxes we ticked. I was always grateful to *The Times* for giving us that line."

Back in New Zealand, anyone who took an interest would have noticed that Air New Zealand was now "flying to London direct from New Zealand". What might not have occurred to them was that Air New Zealand was also "flying to New Zealand direct from London".

There needed to be a market at each end so seats could be filled going both ways. For the journey north, fortunately, there were so many expatriate Britons in New Zealand that there was a large readymade VFR – "Visiting Friends and Relatives" – market.

But New Zealand also had to be marketed and sold as a destination for British travellers. This was not quite such an easy sell, but it was one Air New Zealand would take on with gusto – once it secured the route. Between 1982-1986 there were 384 flights; the figure for the years 1998-2012 was 5096 flights. And to this day Britons are still flying one of Air New Zealand's most popular and successful routes.

Home comforts

Making itself comfortable in the premium-service end of the market, Air New Zealand established the Koru Club, offering seasoned travellers the comforts of home – even when on the other side of the world.

Top New lounge for first- and Pacific-class passengers at Tom Bradley International Terminal, Los Angeles, 1984.

Above The Koru logo.

If Ansett hadn't moved into the New Zealand market, there might never have been a Koru Lounge (or air bridges or valet parking). As Grant Lilly, then Route Manager Domestic, explains: "When we knew Ansett was planning to set up in the New Zealand market, Norman Geary, who was chief executive of Air New Zealand at the time, asked me to develop a plan to prepare for domestic competition. At that time we had none."

New Zealand had a "simple, no-frills, low-cost" airline, but by then the two competing Australian airlines had developed a higher standard of product and service culture at a higher cost. "They had lounges, air bridges and valet parking," says Lilly. "[We knew] Ansett would probably come with that model and look to roll over the top of Air New Zealand in the premium-service end, and those are the most valuable customers – the regulars and business travellers."

A plan was developed to have those facilities in place before Ansett set up in New Zealand. "We worked with the airport companies to get air bridges at the main airports and to service the main flights. They didn't want to do it so Air New Zealand basically paid for, bought and installed the air bridges and we launched valet parking as an adjunct to the Koru Lounges."

The names Koru Club and Koru Lounge were settled on to reflect the aircrafts' livery and because it was already an established symbol for the company. "It was a name New Zealanders would relate to, and a very New Zealand name against an Australian competitor."

The idea was always to distinguish the Koru with a New Zealand feel. "We wanted relaxed style as opposed to a formal five-star hotel product. Our feeling was you can get that in any major hotel and not know who you're staying with, so from day one the focus was around getting a luxury-lodge or upmarket-bach style."

When the first two Koru Lounges were opened simultaneously in Auckland and Wellington, they offered self-service bars with a decent selection of snacks and light refreshments, as well as (then crucial) phone, fax and photocopy facilities, along with television and teletext.

Initial uptake was strong. "One of the early signs that was good," says Lilly, "was that we launched with annual subs and life memberships, and life memberships sold quickly and well. I still bump into people today who tell me they bought a life membership then, are still travelling and that it was one of the best deals they ever got."

The lounges continue to be popular, with new Koru members joining the programme every year. Stories abound of people leaving early for the airport "and then we can sit in the Koru Lounge". Lilly takes pride in the fact Air New Zealand's members' lounge is more egalitarian than those of its Australian counterparts. "They had normal clubs and a club within a club, an invitation-only one. You paid more for the exclusive part. We decided not to do that and I think it's a great reflection of the more simple style in New Zealand that has worked very well."

Clockwise from left
The Koru lounge
at Sydney Airport;
the Jasmax-
designed lounge
at the refurbished
Christchurch Airport;
Hamilton's Koru lounge;
the view from Dunedin's
lounge, 2008.

Drama at Nadi

The attempted hijack of an Air New Zealand flight at Nadi Airport was thwarted when an enterprising crew member whacked the hijacker over the head with a whisky bottle.

Left Flight Engineer Graeme Walsh.

In 1987, TE24, piloted by Captain Graeme Gleeson, was returning to Auckland from Tokyo when it made a scheduled stop in Nadi to refuel. On board was Flight Engineer Graeme Walsh, who would become the hero of the day, but not before the drama had played out for six hours on the tarmac at Nadi Airport.

Walsh was carrying out routine pre-flight checks on the flight deck during the refueling stop, when he heard someone thumping up the stairs to the 747's cockpit. "Suddenly, someone came through the flight deck door and started to make demands. He said to do as he said or he would blow up the plane."

The hijacker's name was Ahmjed Ali, a Fijian Indian who Walsh recognised as a load sheet master from the planning division.

The doors to the cabin downstairs were still open, and thanks to the quick action of Brian Ruffell, the captain of a second, resting crew on board the aircraft, the passengers were quickly offloaded to safety, which left the pilot and two crew on the flight deck with the hijacker.

Ali was highly agitated, says Walsh, and armed with a paper bag full of explosives made from melanite stolen from a gold mine, which the locals used for dynamiting fish. "He threw one to the captain and said, 'If you don't do as I say, we will blow up.' He was shaking and smoking and holding his lit cigarette rather close to the fuse."

The hijacker's demands changed constantly: "General Rabuka had taken the Fijian parliamentarians out of parliament and was holding them captive. Ali wanted them released. He said he wanted to see them standing in front of the plane – something that would have taken hours to do. Finally he got that down to four MPs who he would recognise."

He also wanted a message broadcast on Fijian radio to tell people to watch for a plane flying overhead which was intended as a protest over the imprisonment, and he demanded that the fuel tanks be filled to maximum so the aircraft could fly him to Libya.

"He didn't know a lot about the physical operations of the aeroplane. He knew where the lights in the cockpit were that showed whether the doors were open or shut. He said when the doors were closed that if the light came on he would blow us up."

Eventually New Zealand Prime Minister David Lange agreed to talk to Ali, so Walsh sat the hijacker in the jumpseat in the cockpit and put the headphones on him. "I said I was going to the toilet. When I came back, here he was sitting with his back to me, trying to talk on the radio. I thought: 'You've got to be a mug to do that.' He wasn't paying any attention to me. He still had the bomb in his hand, and a match at this stage, because he'd run out of cigarettes. He'd told us the fuse had a burn rate of six seconds, so it would have been pretty short notice if he'd lit it.

"I had bought my father a bottle of Teacher's whisky that was sitting in a paper bag in the crew rest area. I went back, picked it up and lashed out, hitting him on the head with the whisky bottle."

Walsh grabbed him and threw him on the floor. "I got on top of him and to stop him from wriggling I put my fingers in the base of his throat and pushed as hard as I could." Between the three of them, the hijacker was subdued and handcuffed, so he was immobile.

"Then I ran down the stairs, opened the door and started yelling, and it was like yelling into a desert. There was no one around. The passengers had been kept in the terminal and the one other plane that had been parked next to us had been shifted away in case anything happened. All the other planes were at least 300-400m away. Then I opened the cabin doors further. Suddenly people came from everywhere and Ali was taken away."

Looking back, says Walsh, there was no doubt it had been a very high-risk situation. "The police took one of the bombs later and put it in an old wreck of a car and detonated it. It completely destroyed the car.

"I was a physical and emotional wreck straight after the ordeal," he says. "I'd never done anything like that before and haven't experienced anything like it since."

The scenic route

Throughout the 80s Air New Zealand focused on consolidating its secondary routes, purchasing shares in the Mount Cook Group, Air Nelson and Eagle Air.

Top A Mount Cook Airlines Britten Norman Islander, Milford Sound Airport.

Right and far right Air Nelson and Eagle Air took over Air New Zealand's regional routes.

Pride and joy

Prime Minister David Lange chats to the chef after the unveiling of the first Boeing 767, *Aotearoa*, at Wellington.

Koru Care begins

Below The head prefect of St Peter's College hands over a cheque for money raised for the Disneyland project.

The children's charity known as Koru Care started in the early 1980s with donations from airline staff funding special flights for disadvantaged kids.

Koru Care is a registered charity initially set up by staff of Air New Zealand for children "who have drawn the short straw". Its first event was a simple trip to the movies in 1983, but two years later it had raised enough money to take a group of youngsters to the UK.

"These days," according to its website, "the Koru Care committee arranges several overseas trips every year for groups of children and caregivers. Our other activities include supplying educational and play equipment, setting up toy libraries, taking children on special day excursions and organising Christmas parties."

The charity was launched with donations from staff – from engineers to catering and every division in between. A small amount was taken out of their pay every week. Koru Care now has other sponsors as well, but fundraising at first was at the cake stall/sausage sizzle level.

"The company gave a certain number of flights and we fundraised for the rest. It was so much fun to see the kids enjoy it. They got to ride on the cane train from Lautoka," says former hostess and Koru Care stalwart Janet Beech.

But Air New Zealand had been going out of its way to create great memories for disadvantaged kids even before Koru Care was established. A memorable account of a trip to California appeared in *Air New Zealand News* for 15 November 1979.

"The 230 children in the group got off to a great start when they found themselves on the same aircraft as the All Blacks, who signed autographs, led sing-alongs and generally made a fuss of them.

"An Auckland businessman, Mike Clarkin, who was also on the flight, rushed into a duty free shop in transit and bought two cartons of toys and trucks for the boys and cuddly koalas for the girls.

"The fuss kept up when they got to LA, with coverage from a local TV news show on the day they arrived and the day after.

"The children, who were accompanied by a TV One crew making a documentary about the 10-day trip, met the owner of Kinny's Great American Shoe store, who was so impressed that he decided to outfit the whole 230 with shoes, socks and T-shirts.

"The TV show *CHiPS* was all the rage then and the children met its star Erik Estrada at the height of his popularity as well as getting a motorcycle escort from the Los Angeles Police Department. Other highlights were visits to Universal Studios and Disneyland.

"The most memorable part of the trip was the bond that grew among the children and their escorts," says one who was there. "It grew stronger with each day until, at the end, there were tears and sorrowful partings. It may have been their trip of a lifetime, but it was ours too."

Private life

A Boeing 737 approaches Wellington Airport over Lyall Bay.

The government's move to privatise Air New Zealand was met with widespread disapproval, but it was also seen as an opportunity to exercise new freedoms within the business. What followed was a future much more firmly focused on financial return.

In June 1987, the free-market-minded Labour Government announced that it would sell 25 percent of its stake in Air New Zealand. The year before, it had opened the domestic market to foreign competitors, unlike its trans-Tasman counterpart, which restricted foreign ownership of domestic airlines to a 15 percent stake.

The ideal form of sale would have been a public sharemarket float, but in the wake of the 1987 market crash, it was deemed that this would not be successful.

Instead, the Government sought a private buyer and Qantas looked likely to be the winning bidder. The thought of an Australian airline buying into the national carrier did not sit well with many, so bidding was opened again with 100 percent of the carrier up for grabs.

Government ownership had been a mixed blessing for Air New Zealand. The Government did not interfere overly in the running of the airline, but it certainly took a keen interest. It was also seen by some to be a helpful partner in matters such as seeking more capital.

"The privatisation period was an unsettling time," says one former executive. "It would free us from ministers making decisions about what we did. We could be quicker on our feet. But you want to know who's going to be owning you. I had to go to the engineering bases and explain the privatisation – there was a lot of unrest about it."

Richard Gates was one of a three-man team looking after due diligence. "We had 18 months of providing information to potential buyers," he says. "You had plenty of window shoppers. We had our advisers and we had the Government's advisers, and we were up and down to government an awful lot. It wasn't that enjoyable."

Eventually, at the end of 1988, the company was sold to Brierley Investments Ltd (BIL), which took 65 percent, and 35 percent was onsold to the New Zealand public, staff and institutional investors. Qantas acquired 19.9 percent and Japan Airlines and American Airlines bought 7.5 percent each. The Government retained a "Kiwishare", which gave it a right of veto over decisions that might not be in the nation's interest, such as deciding not to fly between Auckland and Wellington any more.

There were certain anomalies in the deal, including the fact that competitors Qantas and American Airlines were now part owners. American and Japan Airlines, who were believed to have invested to stop others getting a piece of the pie, sold out their shares quite quickly.

"We did get a bit edgier when we were privatised and a public company," says Roger Poulton, retired General Manager Americas. "We could be a little freer. We really expanded into Asia in a big way. We got a new chief executive, Jim Scott, who said the focus needed to change from North America and Europe to Asia, so we put additional flights there. We started flying to Kuala Lumpur, Bali, Hong Kong, Bangkok and extra places in Japan. A lot of those flights went via Brisbane, so this was the start of our ongoing strategy to become an Australasian airline, which eventually led to the Ansett experience."

One clear difference between the Government as an owner and BIL was that the latter was much more firmly focused on return on investment. Providing a return for the shareholder – the Government – hadn't been a prime task for Air New Zealand until this point; rather, it was to provide strategic air services for the benefit of the country. With privatisation it became more commercialised.

Cross-subsidising routes – using more profitable routes to help pay for less successful ones – was looked at suspiciously. So the airline moved to smaller aircraft, while associated and subsidiary carriers, like Eagle Air and Air Nelson, eventually became wholly owned subsidiaries – though their names were retained because of the local affiliations they had.

The irony of the privatisation experiment was that, although it may have sharpened up the business discipline of the company – which was already successful – it ultimately led to near bankruptcy during the Ansett imbroglio.

(160) **History: 1990–1999**
Milestones and other
memorable moments
from the decade.

(166) **50th anniversary**
How we celebrated our
first half century.

(168) **At your service**
Engineering is one of the
airline's most important
divisions.

(172) **Suits staff down to
the ground**
There's nothing dowdy
about these down-to-
earth styles.

(174) **Where there was
smoke**
A smoking ban is a
breath of fresh air.

(176) **Brand new day**
A massive make-over for
the airline's livery.

(178) **The Ansett tail**
An expansive initiative
proved a costly exercise.

=1999

The last decade of the millennium got off to a great start with the arrival of the first Boeing 747-400 in 1992, and bright new uniforms to go with it. It ended with the airline locked in a battle over control of the Australian airline Ansett, of which it had acquired half in 1995.

Significant developments in between included the extension of a ban on smoking on aircraft. Introduced on domestic flights in the previous decade, it was finally extended to international legs, a move welcomed by most passengers and all crew.

A tourism boom, which saw visitor numbers top one and a quarter million, had considerable flow-on benefits for Air New Zealand.

Organisational changes were a feature of the early years of the decade. The last legacy of TEAL – the TE flight designator – vanished, to be replaced by NZ across all flights. And the entire company was split into six business units: international, domestic, cargo, catering, engineering and information. A new "Pacific Wave"

livery, which retained the Koru, was introduced.

Services to Seoul, Taiwan and Nagoya, followed by Osaka and Fukuoka, in Japan, were introduced. Flights to Kuala Lumpur came to an end. Frequencies were increased on other routes throughout the decade as new aircraft provided more capacity. "Snow Express" flights to Queenstown from Australia became popular in the winter sports season.

The London service moved to daily frequency in 1998, and Air New Zealand joined the international Star Alliance network of airlines in 1999.

The Queen continued her patronage of Air New Zealand, becoming the first monarch to take a regularly scheduled flight when she travelled to Auckland for the Commonwealth Heads of Government Meeting.

In a coup for one of its unsung but most important divisions, the Auckland Engineering base secured a contract for assembling, inspecting and testing gas turbine engines for Australian ANZAC frigates.

A tourism boom, which saw visitor numbers top one and a quarter million, had considerable flow-on benefits for Air New Zealand. Organisational changes were a feature of the early years of the decade.

Above The 1990s sees staff take on a fresh look in uniforms by Barbara Lee.

Top right A new livery is introduced with a "Pacific Wave" formed by two ribbons in the corporate colours.

Right Australia's News Corporation takes control of Ansett New Zealand.

Far right Commemorative stamps celebrate Air New Zealand's 50th anniversary in 1990.

1 April 1990

Air New Zealand and British Airways sign a commercial alliance effectively giving both airlines daily round-the-world services. "Streamline" connections offers flights from the United Kingdom to New Zealand and vice versa on either airline via the east or west.

Below The Fokker F27 Friendship fleet is retired.

Below right Mount Cook Airline is brought in under the Air New Zealand umbrella.

30 April 1990

50th anniversary of the first flight by TEAL to Sydney in 1940.

2 August 1990

Air New Zealand announces that the now uneconomic Fokker F27 Friendship provincial fleet is to be withdrawn.

21 September 1990

For the eighth year running, Air New Zealand is voted the "Best Carrier to the Pacific" by UK-based magazine *Executive Travel*.

18 April 1991

Air New Zealand acquires 100 percent interest in the Mount Cook Group.

21 May 1991

Air New Zealand's domestic airline operations move under the banner of Air New Zealand National, and regional carriers Eagle Air and Air Nelson use the name Air New Zealand Link.

26 August 1991

The airline's Christchurch Engineering base wins export award at the New Zealand Trade and Development Boards Export Awards.

September 1991

After changing its balance date from March 31 to June 30, Air New Zealand announces a consolidated net profit of $5.5 million for the 15-month period to 30 June 1991.

15 September 1991

A group of 175 children with special needs flies from New Zealand to the US as part of "Operation Disneyland", organised by Koru Care, and supported by Air New Zealand.

HISTORICAL EVENTS IN NEW ZEALAND
1990—99

1990
- Dame Catherine Tizard (far left) becomes first woman Governor-General.
- One and two-cent coins are no longer legal tender (left).
- Commonwealth Games held in Auckland.
- Dr Penny Jamieson (right) is made Anglican Bishop of Dunedin, becoming the world's first female diocesan bishop.

22 January 1992

The airline opens a multilingual Eurolink reservations centre in Antwerp to handle telephone bookings from France, Germany, Italy, Spain, Portugal, Benelux and Scandinavian countries.

24 January 1992

Auckland Engineering base wins contract to assemble, inspect and test 11 General Motors LM2500 gas turbine engines for Australian ANZAC frigates.

February 1992

American Airlines sells its stake in Air New Zealand.

25 November 1992

Air New Zealand wins the "Most Improved Performance" section of the *Deloitte/Management* magazine Top 200 business awards.

22 July 1993

Commencement of operations by Terminal Services New Zealand, a business unit which provides ground handling, loading, engineering and line maintenance services at Auckland, Wellington and Christchurch for the Air New Zealand Group and to airline customers.

2 September 1993

Air New Zealand wins Cellar in the Sky international wine competition.

1 December 1993

Air New Zealand acquires 100 percent shareholding in Eagle Aviation Limited (Eagle Airways).

January 1994

United Kingdom travel agents and travel industry members vote Air New Zealand "Best Airline to the Pacific" in a poll by *Travel Weekly* magazine.

16 May 1994

Official launch of the company's sponsorship of New Zealand's major rugby competition, the National Provincial Championship.

Below Air New Zealand sponsorship of NPC kicks off with referee uniforms and flags bearing the company logo.

1991
- The Resource Management Act 1991 is enacted, rewriting planning law.
- New Zealand troops join multinational force in the Gulf War.
- An avalanche on Aoraki/Mount Cook (right) reduces its height by 10.5m.
- 1193 New Zealanders are now connected to the internet.

1992
- New Zealand gets seat on United Nations Security Council.
- Student-loan system is started and tertiary fees raised.
- Barbara Kendall is the sole New Zealand gold medal winner at the Barcelona Olympics (right).
- "Big Snow" in Canterbury kills more than one million sheep.

1993
- Referendum favours MMP electoral system.
- Opposition MP Peter Tapsell becomes Speaker of the House, thus giving the government a majority.

1990–1999

21 December 1994
Japan Airlines (JAL) sells its shares in Air New Zealand to Brierley Investments Ltd. JAL has been a shareholder in Air New Zealand since April 1989.

24 May 1995
America's Cup winning team arrives home in Auckland on board special Air New Zealand Boeing 767 flight from the United States.

5 September 1995
Air New Zealand reports an after-tax net consolidated surplus of $260 million for 1994-95 – a 36 percent improvement on the 1993-94 year.

1 November 1995
Her Majesty Queen Elizabeth II lands in Auckland aboard Air New Zealand flight NZ1 from London via Los Angeles, to attend the Commonwealth Heads of Government Meeting. This was the first routine commercial flight used by a reigning British monarch.

17 November 1995
Air New Zealand announces its intention to seek a shareholding in Ansett Australia.

8 December 1995
Launch of Freedom Air International, operating low-cost flights between New Zealand and Australia.

31 December 1995
Air New Zealand takes 100 percent stake in Air New Zealand Link operator Air Nelson (formerly 50 percent owned).

Far left The first reigning British monarch to travel on a routine commercial flight, Queen Elizabeth II leaves the Air New Zealand aircraft.

Left A triumphant Team New Zealand returns from the America's Cup on a special homecoming flight.

1994
- New Zealand's first casino opens in Christchurch.
- Jane Campion and Anna Paquin (right) win Oscars for *The Piano*.

1995
- Team New Zealand wins America's Cup (left).
- The Auckland Warriors play their first match in the NSW Rugby League's expanded Winfield Cup competition.

- Waikato-Tainui is the first iwi to reach an historic Treaty of Waitangi settlement with the Crown (right).

Below One of the Boeing 737-300s set to replace the fleet of 737-200s.

29 April 1996

Air New Zealand announces a new corporate image incorporating the "Pacific Wave". The well-known Koru is retained, and adapted.

2 September 1996

Air New Zealand enters into an agreement to acquire 50 percent of the Ansett Holdings Limited Group for $540 million, providing Air New Zealand with a stake in the Australian aviation market.

December 1996

Trial begins of Electronic Ticketing on domestic services, ushering in ticketless travel.

26 June 1997

Decision made to make all international flights smoke-free from 1 November, following government ratification of an international treaty.

21 January 1998

Air New Zealand wins gold medal as best business class carrier and for the best check-in staff at the 1998 *Executive Travel* magazine awards.

17 April 1998

The airline becomes a sponsor of the America's Cup 2000 campaign and official carrier to the Team New Zealand syndicate.

28 October 1998

Plans announced to commence replacement of domestic jet fleet, starting October 1999. New Boeing 737-300s will progressively replace the existing fleet of Boeing 737-200s.

9 November 1998

Services between London and Auckland move to daily frequency, 16 years after the first flights by Air New Zealand on this route.

21 January 1999

Air New Zealand reclaims prestigious Globe award as "Best Airline to the Pacific" from Qantas, having previously won four years in succession (1994-97). Voted by readers of UK's *Travel Weekly*.

6 April 1999

Air New Zealand announces the sale of light-aircraft operations and coach-touring business of subsidiary Mt Cook Group Ltd to Tourism Holdings.

3 May 1999

Air New Zealand and Ansett Australia join the Star Alliance network.

16 December 1999

Defibrillators introduced on international aircraft.

1996
- First MMP election brings National/New Zealand First coalition government (right).

1997
- Jim Bolger resigns as Prime Minister after losing support of the National Party caucus, and is replaced by New Zealand's first woman Prime Minister, Jenny Shipley (left).
- Auckland's Sky Tower is opened.
- Beatrice Faumuina wins gold in the discus at the World Championships in Athletics.

1998
- Auckland city businesses hit by a power cut lasting several weeks.
- The women's rugby team, the Black Ferns, become the world champions (right).

1999
- Alcohol purchase age for off-licences reduced from 20 to 18 years of age.
- Trade Me is founded.

On 30 April 1940 the first commercial flight was made by a TEAL flying boat, taking nine passengers on a 10-hour journey from Auckland to Sydney. Half a century and many milestones later, Air New Zealand celebrated how far it had come.

Above left An anniversary poster proclaiming "Fifty Years of Excellence" is installed.

Left Air New Zealand Singapore staff cut the anniversary cake.

1990–1999

Air New Zealand's 1999 ad campaign, "The World's Warmest Welcome", is an instant hit with the New Zealand public.

AIR NEW ZEALAND
The world's warmest welcome

TEAL staff work on plane engines inside a workshop, 1946.

At your service

Air New Zealand's highly skilled team of aircraft engineers provide world-technical experience that means their services are sought by other international airlines too – providing a valuable revenue stream for the company.

Engineering services is one of Air New Zealand's key divisions, responsible not only for maintaining its own aircraft but also as a revenue stream with contracts to maintain other airlines' aircraft.

"If you ask an engineer we will tell you the aircraft is ours and we lend them to the pilots to fly," explains head of engineering Grant Crenfeldt. "We think of them as having personalities because they all have little quirks and foibles – we get to know them over a period of time." It's the maintenance division's job to provide a safe, reliable, compliant and cost-effective aircraft, and to meet the schedule the airline wants to fly.

That mission statement covers a host of varied activities that stretch into all aspects of the airline's business. When Air New Zealand purchases an aircraft, the engineers consider what air conditioning or heating requirements are needed in the cargo holds, but they are also intimately involved with the passenger experience, since they are responsible for standards in the cabin, such as inflight entertainment services.

When an aircraft has been ordered and is being built, Air New Zealand will always have someone on hand at the manufacturer to keep an eye on its investment, and get involved in the process – the airline routinely makes large changes to the interior of its aircraft, for example, rebuilding it into something unique – and the majority of that work is done by New Zealanders.

The company's engineers also work on line maintenance and overhaul. "In line maintenance, you have a general understanding of the whole thing," says Kevin Berry, who has spent much of his time working in maintenance since joining the company in 1964: when he started at TEAL, the first aircraft he worked on were flying boats. Overhaul is broken down into structures, systems, and avionics; increasingly there are specialties such as composites – fibre glass and carbon fibre.

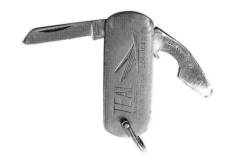

Top Pontoons are unloaded in Auckland in 1939, ready to receive TEAL's first aircraft.

Above TEAL staff service a Solent aircraft at Mechanics Bay, Auckland, 1949.

Right A TEAL-branded pocketknife.

Maintenance work contracted for other airlines is a strong revenue stream to this day – the airline has around 25 key customers: most are other airlines, but not all. Air New Zealand carries out all the Australian domestic airlines' work under contract and often you could find two or three 747s being worked on at Christchurch International.

Where many airlines have reduced their overheads by contracting out maintenance, Air New Zealand has done the opposite: because of the country's remoteness the airline has turned maintenance into a source of revenue. The two maintenance bases in Auckland and Christchurch market themselves aggressively, and the airline's reputation as a maintenance provider on engines, air frames and avionics is up there with the best in the world.

Naturally, rapidly changing technology has a huge impact. Thirty years ago all the flight controls moved by cables from the control column. On an aircraft designed in the mid-1980s, there were 300 pieces of software loaded into components. On a new 787 there are about 1300.

The world has taken notice of the quality of Air New Zealand's engineering. "We are highly respected in the industry despite being a small airline compared to others," says Crenfeldt. "We constantly have airframe or engine manufacturers sending us their graduates for further training. In any one year we would have two to five people from Boeing, Airbus or Rolls-Royce working with us."

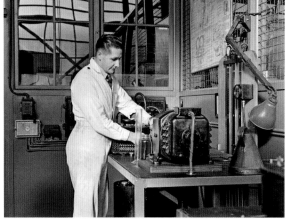

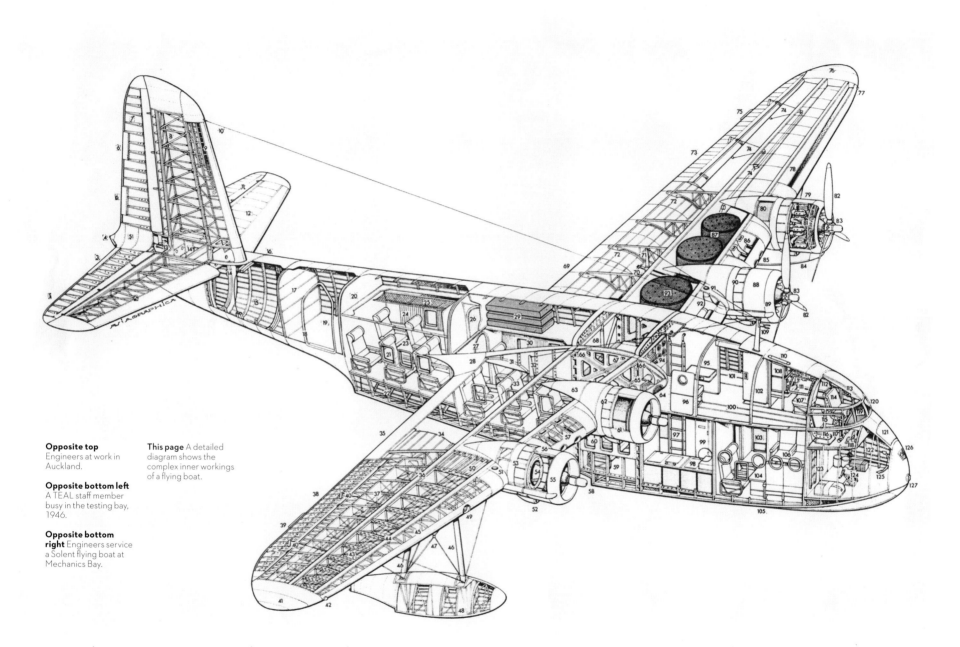

Opposite top
Engineers at work in
Auckland.

Opposite bottom left
A TEAL staff member
busy in the testing bay,
1946.

**Opposite bottom
right** Engineers service
a Solent flying boat at
Mechanics Bay.

This page A detailed
diagram shows the
complex inner workings
of a flying boat.

Suits staff down to the ground

Opposite and below
The new Barbara Lee uniform was unveiled in 1992.

A new ground-staff wardrobe designed by Barbara Lee, of Christchurch, and introduced in 1992, completed the project of making the same overall corporate style available for the first time in the airline's 53-year history. The new ground-staff wardrobe was the first change for 1200 staff based at airports, travel centres and airline offices around the world. The women's wardrobe featured a collection of tailored and print separates in Pacific jade and dark navy blue, while the men wore jackets in Pacific jade, with navy trousers, and a tie featuring the Koru motif.

In 1998, Lee also designed uniforms for Air New Zealand Koru Club and First Class Lounge Customer Liaison Officers. They were predominantly navy blue, with touches of Air New Zealand's corporate teal colour. The women's uniform contained four basic outfits allowing for a range of mix-and-match options. The male uniform was given the addition of a new tie and a matching handkerchief, and a gold Koru badge.

Where there was smoke

Below left An Air New Zealand brand lighter.

Below right and bottom Signs direct passengers into smoking or no-smoking areas – although the line between sections was somewhat hazy.

In the early days of flying, smoking was permitted on all flights. Decades later, the decision to ban the practice on planes was a breath of fresh air for passengers and crew alike.

It's one of those things people now find hard to believe ever happened. Aircraft used to have smoking "sections" in which people were allowed to smoke cigarettes. This meant that the cabin was in two blocks. At a certain point, there was a last row of non-smokers. Behind that, the first of several rows in which people could smoke. There was nothing to prevent the smoke drifting into the non-smoking section and the practice of smoking on board was unpleasant for just about everyone except the most diehard nicotine addicts.

Smoking wasn't just confined to the passenger sections. "When I joined the company," says a retired pilot, "there were only about three of us who didn't smoke. The flight deck was a constant fug. Around the outflow valves of the pressurisation system there was this mucky mess of nicotine stain and residue that had gone through the system. I used to come home from a week flying across the Tasman and hang my uniform on the line to get rid of the smell."

The acceptance of smoking extended to branded company ashtrays to complement the in-flight ashtrays that lingered in aircraft long after smoking had been prohibited.

The ban came after several years of agitation for it. In 1991, the World Health Organization launched a smoke-free skies campaign urging the International Civil Aviation Organization to make all member countries smoke-free. "There [is] an urgent need for Air New Zealand to address the problem and admit that its employees and passengers are affected as it is not possible in an aircraft to cater for hundreds of smokers and non-smokers, as the smoke spreads throughout the whole aircraft," said Dr Michael Carr-Gregg, then Executive Director of the New Zealand Drug Foundation.

"Air New Zealand Cabin Crew working on international flights [a]re not protected from the effects of Environmental Tobacco smoke, as all areas are affected by smoke-polluted air."

The change was almost universally welcomed by crew when on 31 March 1995 all flights – except those to Japan and Korea, to which the ban was extended later – became smoke-free.

If you wish to smoke during your flight please ask for a seat in the 'smoking area' when you check-in

◆ NAC WINGS OF THE NATION

AIR NEW ZEALAND

NO SMOKING SECTION THIS SIDE

Left A TEAL Senior Steward on the Solent lighting passengers' cigarettes, 1953.

Above An in-flight duty-free list prices cigarettes at 30c each. Air New Zealand lighters were also available.

175

Brand new day

Rebranding an airline can be a challenging and sensitive exercise, especially when the company is so close to its nation's heart. Air New Zealand has undertaken the task three times, with the most extensive makeover taking effect in the mid-1990s.

In the beginning, NAC and TEAL both had stylised bird logos. Design writer Michael Smythe once observed that the former's godwit, a bird known for its long-distance flights, was not the best fit for a domestic airline. TEAL's maroro or flying fish was probably better suited to an airline that began its life with a fleet of flying boats.

TEAL became Air New Zealand in 1965 but it was a few years before the decision was taken to move to a jet-age logo. Agencies were briefed, but none of the initial submissions was accepted – though suggestions that the ultimate choice should have a Pacific theme were taken seriously.

At Roundhill Studios, artists Ken Chapman and Tom Elliott between them developed the design that would eventually become the Koru. At first it was "an arrow form which was shaped as a fern frond [with] three wavy lines under to suggest the ocean".

The first Roundhill effort didn't work out but with the "ocean" dropped and the "arrow" redesigned, the pair devised what would become one of the most respected and enduring logos in the country's history. The Koru was superbly apt, a stylised fern frond that in Maori iconography represents new life and is indeed to be found carved on waka. A DC-10 bearing the Koru was unveiled in January 1973. It has thus been part of the Air New Zealand brand for more than 40 years.

In the mid-1990s the airline was ready for a new look. Their hunt would turn into what may have been the biggest design project ever undertaken in New Zealand. After three years and one false start, the company settled on a British design firm, Davies Baron. Their job was to help establish Air New Zealand as an internationally recognised brand. Local firm Dave Clark Design Associates was hired to help provide local context to the designers half a world away.

It would prove a challenging process, massive in scale and not helped by the distances involved. Technology has come a long way since then – although both ends took advantage of email to transmit files across the globe, when they sent an email, they would also send a fax to let the

Above, from top TEAL Short Solent with flying fish logo; the NAC logo featured the stylised godwit; TEAL becomes Air New Zealand and aircraft now featured the Southern Cross on the tail and the maroro on the upper fusilage.

Far left The Koru was introduced with the DC-10 in 1973.

Left The Koru was retained, and the "Pacific Wave" was added to the livery.

Below The Silver Fern logo is added to the fusilage.

other end know it was on its way.

The redesign would cover everything Air New Zealand owned – the interior and exterior of its aircraft, offices, vehicles, stationery, crockery, glassware, uniforms, fabrics… Staff were consulted early on to ensure their support and it soon became clear that the TEAL colour scheme and the Koru had to stay in there somewhere.

Ultimately, the key element in the new livery – the "Pacific Wave" of two stylised ribbons in the traditional brand colours – reflected an outsider's perspective. It arose from the British designers' impression of Pacific sea and sky in the New Zealand environment. The new livery achieved its purpose of updating a tired look without turning its back on the past.

The next major change came in 2011 when Air New Zealand painted an A320 aircraft black to support the All Blacks, of whom they were a sponsor, in the Rugby World Cup in New Zealand the same year. This was the only black aircraft in the world and attracted much international attention. The following year a rebrand was announced that would see a new black livery adopted across the fleet. Most aircraft would be white with a black tail, but a few would be black with white tails.

The airline was also given permission by Tourism New Zealand and New Zealand Trade and Enterprise to use their silver fern logo alongside the Koru. "The driving idea was 'flying the flag for New Zealand,'" according to Designworks, the company Air New Zealand engaged for the project. "We used the iconic silver fern as our inspiration. It was already a powerful and internationally recognised symbol with brand equity we could leverage. And fittingly, it was the New Zealand tourism symbol – its use signifying opening the world to New Zealand. The design is flexible and simple, allowing it to be scaled across the fleet."

The first Boeing 787-9 aircraft bearing the airline's distinctive new all-black livery was revealed at Boeing's Everett factory near Seattle in April 2014. It was the first 787-9 to go into service and thus a fitting "canvas" for the new livery which complements the white and black livery on certain aircraft.

The Ansett tail

In 1995, the long-standing aspiration for Air New Zealand to expand into the much larger Australian market finally began to come to fruition. The opportunity to build an Australasian network to rival Qantas began with the purchase of the first half of Ansett early in 1996. The second half was acquired in 2000, but just over a year later the dream was over. Air New Zealand announced the biggest loss in New Zealand corporate history and amid job losses and media frenzy, Ansett was shut down.

There were many players and many events that contributed to the debacle that was Air New Zealand's investment in Ansett. Many were beyond the control of Air New Zealand but it has to be acknowledged that this was not its finest hour.

Air New Zealand's involvement in Ansett had many twists and turns, not least in the origin of the decision to make the ill-fated investment. It had long been recognised that the ability of Air New Zealand to grow its business from a population base of just under four million New Zealanders was seriously limited. The obvious growth path was expansion to Australia, but that was blocked by the lack of traffic rights in the domestic Australian market.

A study of that market lead Air New Zealand to decide that the duopoly of Ansett and Qantas could best be challenged by the-then novel concept of a "low-cost airline". This strategy had been successfully launched against large established carriers in the domestic US market by Southwest Airlines, and a confidential plan code-named NZX was hatched. This progressed in parallel with political discussions to establish an open-skies Single Aviation Market for New Zealand and Australia, which would include rights for New Zealand airlines to operate in the Australian domestic market. (Ansett had been operating in New Zealand since 1987.)

Following the sale of Air New Zealand by the Government in 1987, its shareholders included Qantas with a 19.9 percent holding, and three Qantas directors also sat on the Air New Zealand board. As the planned announcement of the Single Aviation Agreement by the Australian and New Zealand politicians in September 1994 approached, the NZX plan was revealed to the board. Very shortly thereafter, a facsimile was received in Wellington from Hon Laurie Brereton, the Australian Minister of Transport, advising that the Single Aviation Market would not proceed.

In the following months, it became clear to Air New Zealand's board that if they wanted to participate in the Australian market there was a major shareholder of Ansett that would like to exit its investment – but negotiations with News Corp failed over the small matter of price. On hearing that, the other 50 percent shareholder, TNT, said that it would be happy to sell and so the first 50 percent of Ansett was purchased in November 1996 for A$425 million.

The next four years were spent sitting on the board, but in the back seat, of an airline which under a shareholders' agreement was managed by News Corp appointee, Rod Eddington. Ansett's deep-seated problems were all too evident: an old and mixed fleet, high staff and other costs and a

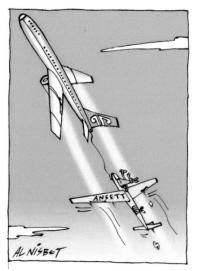

competitor able to under-price it on key routes. A very loyal customer base kept Ansett going but clearly things had to change and the other shareholder was not about to put up any more capital to address the issues.

Matters crystallised in March 1999 when, to Air New Zealand's utter disbelief, *The Age* newspaper in Melbourne featured a handshake deal between News Corp and Singapore Airlines for News Corp to sell its half of Ansett. A sensitive discussion occurred later that day when Air New Zealand politely reminded News Corp that as part of the TNT deal (which gave News Corp management control and the addition of A$150 million capital to Ansett by Air New Zealand) News Corp had granted a pre-emptive right to Air New Zealand to purchase News Corp's shares in Ansett if News decided to sell. Air New Zealand now proposed to exercise its right.

The negotiated purchase from News Corp, completed in June 2000 for A$580 million, also saw Singapore Airlines purchase 25 percent of Air New Zealand shares from Brierley Investments, appointing three directors to the Air New Zealand board. The building blocks were in place with a strategic airline partner to help re-equip the ageing Ansett fleet and rebuild the airline.

But life doesn't always work out as planned, and so it was with Ansett. Now with full control, management set about a strategy to integrate the two businesses into an Australasian airline. As that process evolved, the depth of problems at Ansett became increasingly apparent. The fleet wasn't just old, the engineering work had developed a serious backlog, meaning aircraft had to be taken out of service at short notice. Consequent cancellations, delays and re-scheduling saw once-loyal customers lose patience. Staff were not quick to relish the prospect of integration with their Kiwi cousins and the unions were unimpressed by many of the integration plans.

A cruel irony appeared in August 2000 with the arrival in the domestic market of Richard Branson's Virgin media machine and a low-cost airline, Virgin Blue. Suddenly Ansett was battling not just the established scale of Qantas in the business and leisure markets but a new competitor with even lower costs attacking the low-fare end of the market. It was in no man's land.

A crucial point was reached at Easter of 2001. What was to have been the highest revenue and passenger numbers day in Ansett's history turned to disaster as its Boeing 767 fleet was grounded suddenly by CASA, which expressed safety concerns. This followed a previous grounding of the B767 fleet in December 2000 right on Christmas due to maintenance errors.

Ultimately, Ansett was able to satisfy all of CASA's concerns and show that the aircraft were safe to operate, but a severe wound had been inflicted financially and, more importantly, on Ansett's reputation.

At the same time Qantas was in a favourable fuel-hedging position as the fuel price began to rise significantly and enjoyed a cost advantage over Ansett. That wasn't lost on Qantas which, like any good competitor, wasn't about to remove its foot from Ansett's throat while there was any sign of life.

The groundings had caused significant damage and weekly losses were mounting. A recovery strategy was needed urgently and the proposal put to the Air New Zealand board was the purchase of Virgin Blue. The combined airlines with Virgin's lower cost base could buy time and recover some market share. Richard Branson was reportedly willing to sell for A$100 million. Regulatory approval was needed and an initial sounding was taken from Professor Alan Fels, then the Chairman of the ACCC. Approval is often given on the basis that without a merger, one of the two businesses will inevitably fail. Virgin Blue was still a small start-up airline in a market littered with start-up failures. Professor Fels was visibly shocked when informed that the failure could be Ansett.

Between May and August of 2000 various recapitalisations were considered by the board but against a backdrop of required regulatory approvals and shareholders' faltering confidence, the plans (with the benefit of hindsight) were not proceeding with the pace they needed to. Those months gave Virgin Blue breathing room as Ansett continued to deteriorate. Branson was not unaware of this and by August was sufficiently confident in Virgin Blue's future to very publicly tear up an offer for A$250 million.

Time was already running out when the accounting rules played their hand. Air New Zealand's accounts had to be filed and that required valuation of assets, including fleet, to be based on a "going concern" business. At that point the options for recovery were exhausted. Air New Zealand, which had itself remained profitable while funnelling over A$100 million into Ansett since January, would be dragged under by the Ansett anchor unless the unthinkable was done.

Late on the infamous 11 September 2001, time ran out as the Air New Zealand board faced the reality that there was no option but to appoint administrators for Ansett the following day. Even later that night, at 3.40am, an Air New Zealand executive received a call from United Airlines reporting that a UA/NZ code-shared aircraft had crashed into one of the World Trade Centre towers in New York.

The aviation world had become surreal.

184 **History: 2000–2009**
Milestones and other memorable moments from the decade.

190 **Reversal of fortune**
A corporate shake-up and new direction pull Air New Zealand out of its post-Ansett slump.

194 **Switching gear**
Introduction of Zambesi-designed uniforms.

196 **Fun and games**
The evolution of entertainment in the skies.

198 **In the seat pocket in front of you**
From *TEAL South Pacific* to today's *KiaOra*, inflight magazines have taken many forms.

200 **Coming back down to earth**
The Air New Zealand Trust takes action to restore Aotearoa's natural beauty.

202 **What a joke**
A selection of cartoons and comics showing the airline through artists' eyes.

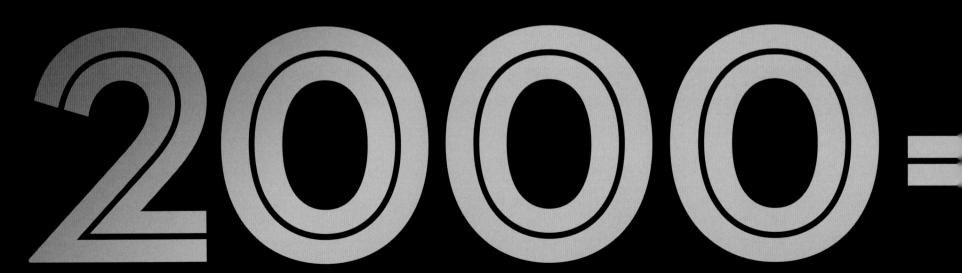

=2009

The start of the new millennium was dominated by wrangling over Ansett and rising fuel prices, but by the end of the decade, Air New Zealand would be a radically different airline after introducing new product, new aircraft, new destinations and – most importantly – a bold new vision for the future.

Air New Zealand had acquired 100 percent ownership of the Australian carrier Ansett, and it soon became a millstone. In 2001, just days after the international aviation industry was rocked by the 9/11 attacks on the United States, Ansett was put into administration before going out of business entirely. Air New Zealand was pummelled with a $1.4 billion operating loss.

Things could only get better – and they did. Having teetered on the brink of bankruptcy in the wake of Ansett, the airline was renationalised by the government at the last minute and, its fortunes secure, set about a programme of modernisation and expansion.

It ordered new Airbus A320, Boeing 777 and 787 aircraft and by 2003 was back in the black, with improved profits in the following years.

The first of the company's entertaining safety videos – this one featuring crew in body paint – debuted in 2009. This video and its successors garnered worldwide media and online attention.

The airline also recognised that the future of the aviation industry was tied to better use of natural resources and embarked on a series of experiments aimed at reducing fuel consumption, which also had the bonus side effect of improving the balance sheet.

A key development in these years was a focus on customer offerings, with new pricing plans, meal options, luggage packages and cheap online booking services. The total of $1 million in one day for online bookings was reached soon after their introduction.

And as it introduced new seating arrangements, class structures and beverage plans – as well new state-of-the art check-in systems – the airline began flying to new destinations around the Asia-Pacific region, including Vancouver and Shanghai. The turnaround was underway.

As it introduced new seating arrangements, class structures and beverage plans – as well new state-of-the art check-in systems – the airline began flying to new destinations around the Asia-Pacific region, including Vancouver and Shanghai.

Above and top right Air New Zealand threw its weight behind Peter Jackson's Middle-earth with innovative campaigns that included aircraft liveries featuring stars such as Liv Tyler.

Right New domestic self check-in kiosks are introduced.

Far right A performer dressed in drag for the annual Pink Flight taking revellers to Sydney's Mardi Gras.

2000–2009

January 2000
Air New Zealand named Best Airline to the Pacific in the annual *Travel Weekly* Globe awards.

18 February 2000
Air New Zealand announces conditional purchase of the remaining 50 percent of Ansett Holdings Limited.

7 July 2000
MD and CEO Jim McCrea leaves Air New Zealand. Board Chairman Sir Selwyn Cushing assumes role of Executive Chairman.

October 2000
An official Olympics carrier, Air New Zealand experiences its busiest day at Sydney International Airport in 60 years with 30 flights taking Olympic Games visitors home.

5 March 2001
ANNZES wins $180 million engine maintenance contract for El Paso Corporation, the largest natural gas company in the world.

28 March 2001
New round-the-world cargo freighter service launched by Air New Zealand Cargo in conjunction with Lufthansa.

21 April 2001
Tasman Pacific's operation, Qantas New Zealand, goes into receivership leaving thousands of New Zealand domestic passengers seeking alternative flight arrangements. Air New Zealand moves instantly to provide extra capacity. Some 18,000 additional passengers are carried in the first three days.

30 April 2001
Joint venture between ANNZES and global engine manufacturers Pratt and Whitney announced, creating the Christchurch Engine Centre.

2 May 2001
Air New Zealand subsidiary Freedom Air begins no-frills domestic main-trunk operation in New Zealand in response to the need for additional domestic flights.

29 May 2001
Qantas Airways Limited approaches Air New Zealand to consider the development of a transaction which would involve the acquisition by Qantas of a significant shareholding in Air New Zealand from Brierley Investments Limited and Singapore Airlines Limited.

7 September 2001
Losses by Ansett Group reach $1.3 million per day.

10 September 2001
Air New Zealand proposes sale of Ansett Australia businesses to Qantas.

12 September 2001
Following the 9/11 attacks, US airspace is closed. One Air New Zealand Boeing 747-400 remains on the ground in Los Angeles, and one in London. Two other aircraft turn back while en route to US airspace.

HISTORICAL EVENTS IN NEW ZEALAND
2000–2009

2000
· Y2K computer rollover fails to cause global or local collapse (right).

2001
· Interest accrual is removed from student loans while studying. Students who accrued interest before 2001 are still required to pay.

· Kiwibank is established.

· Air New Zealand bailout, government purchases a 76.5 percent share in the company.

Below The Christchurch Engine Centre is established, 2001.

Bottom The first A320 aircraft arrives at Auckland International Airport.

13 September 2001
Air New Zealand announces a net loss (after tax, earnings from associates and unusual items) for the financial year to 30 June of $1.425 billion, mainly arising from losses by the Ansett Group.

14 September 2001
Ansett Australia placed into voluntary administration. Australian trade unions retaliate by blockading Air New Zealand aircraft in Australia.

17 December 2001
Last day of commercial operations for the Boeing 737-200 after 33 years' service, mainly on domestic routes. Some 30 aircraft owned or leased over that period are estimated to have made more than 825,000 flights, flying a total distance equivalent to 427 flights to the moon and back.

25 January 2002
Introduction of Air New Zealand Express Class, a range of cheap domestic fares that can only be booked through the internet, initially for services between Auckland, Wellington and Christchurch.

17 May 2002
Air New Zealand cabin crew voted the best in the Pacific region and Australia by a Skytrax customer survey.

July 2002
Grabaseat, Air New Zealand's website featuring daily specials and limited offers, goes live.

1 November 2002
First day of domestic Express Class flights. Enhancements include electronic kiosks for self check-in at major airports and a delay notification service to mobile phones.

15 January 2003
Air New Zealand breaks the million-dollar barrier for a single day's online bookings.

28 August 2003
Air New Zealand announces a profit of $220.3 million, up $187.3 million (567 percent) on the previous financial year.

9 September 2003
The Australian Competition and Consumer Commission (ACCC) turns down the application by Air New Zealand and Qantas to form a strategic alliance.

2002
· Ban on breeding, sale and distribution of ferrets.

2003
· Population of New Zealand exceeds four million.
· Appeals to the Judicial Committee of the Privy Council abolished; Supreme Court of New Zealand established.

2004
· Foreshore and Seabed Act passed.
· Civil Union Act passed (right).
· Maori TV begins broadcasting.

2005
· Prince William arrives in New Zealand for his first visit since he was nine months old.
· Former Prime Minister David Lange dies.

· The Napier landmark statue Pania of the Reef is stolen but recovered eight days later.

16 September 2003
Air New Zealand officially takes delivery of the first of its A320 aircraft from Airbus at a special ceremony in Toulouse, France.

20 December 2003
Air New Zealand's fully owned subsidiary airline, Air Nelson, welcomes a new 33-seat Saab aircraft to its fleet, bringing the total number to 17 Saab-340A aircraft.

28 January 2004
A four-year-old from Christchurch becomes the millionth Airpoints member to sign up for the Air New Zealand frequent-flyer scheme.

19 March 2004
Wanaka becomes the 25th destination in the national network.

22 April 2004
Announcement of Air New Zealand as naming rights sponsor for New Zealand Fashion Week.

June 2004
Purchase of eight Boeing 777-200s, two B787s, and a pending upgrade of the B747s' cabins.

28 June 2004
Air New Zealand unveils its new long-haul product with lie-flat beds, direct-aisle access and audio-video-on-demand in all cabins.

16 September 2004
Condé Nast Traveller UK readers vote Air New Zealand Best Long-haul Airline.

25 January 2005
Air New Zealand raises more than $200,000 in an online airfare auction to aid victims of the Asian tsunami.

1 February 2005
Air New Zealand and the New Zealand Rugby Union sign a four-year sponsorship agreement covering all of the NZRU's teams and tournaments.

4 April 2005
Launch of online integrated holiday packages where customers can choose their own flights, accommodation, transfers, car rental and sightseeing options.

13 July 2006
Air New Zealand Cup rugby competition launched.

Top A flight takes off from Wanaka, Air New Zealand's 25th domestic destination.

Above Lie-flat beds are introduced in Business Class on long-haul flights.

2006
- Five-cent coins are dropped from circulation and existing 10 cent, 20 cent and 50 cent coins are replaced with smaller coins.

- South Island population reaches one million.
- The government announces $11.5 billion surplus, the largest in the country's history and second only to Denmark in the Western World.

- New Zealanders Kevin Biggar and Jamie Fitzgerald walk to the South Pole, the first people to do so carrying their own supplies.

2007
- Willie Apiata (right) becomes the first New Zealander since World War II to be awarded a VC.
- KiwiSaver retirement savings scheme introduced.

6 November 2006
Air New Zealand introduces direct flights to Shanghai.

14 February 2007
Air New Zealand's on-board wine selection scoops the pool in the prestigious UK *Business Traveller* magazine Cellars in the Sky competition.

6 June 2007
Online sales surpass $1 billion for the first time within a financial year.

27 August 2007
RNZAF awards $110 million defence maintenance contract to Air New Zealand subsidiary Safe Air.

11 September 2007
Air Nelson announces it will expand its fleet, purchasing two new Bombardier Q300 aircraft to boost capacity for regional centres.

2 November 2007
First direct flights to Vancouver.

29 January 2008
Air Transport World magazine votes Air New Zealand best passenger-service airline.

27 March 2008
Environment Trust formed to fund research and development into alternative fuels and support projects that enhance New Zealand's clean, green reputation.

28 October 2008
State-of-the-art new domestic check-in experience unveiled, including a new layout, self-check kiosks and new gate scanners for straight-to-gate check-in.

28 November 2008
Air New Zealanders Captain Brian Horrell, Murray White, Michael Gyles and Noel Marsh are lost in an aircraft crash off the coast of Perpignan, France.

10 May 2009
The "Nothing to Hide" TV ad campaign goes live, featuring Air New Zealanders in full body paint.

9 June 2009
Air New Zealand achieves Environmental Gold accreditation, recognising it as one of New Zealand's most environmentally responsible tourism businesses.

26 June 2009
"Bare Essentials" inflight safety video goes live. The video, featuring Air New Zealanders in full body paint, receives more than three million YouTube hits in the next 10 days.

It began the 2000s at an all-time low, but by the end of the decade Air New Zealand was winning accolades as one of the most innovative airlines in the world.

2000–2009

Reversal of fortune

After posting the biggest loss in New Zealand corporate history, Air New Zealand implemented new measures that would see its profits and reputation improve steadily to make it one of the world's most respected and commercially successful airlines.

Like any business, Air New Zealand has been through its commercial ups and downs. In the 1980s, the introduction of new aircraft and routes saw its fortunes improve steadily. Then came Ansett and near bankruptcy, compounded by the 9/11 attacks and the threat of SARS (severe acute respiratory syndrome). Perhaps inevitably, in the financial year that included the Ansett collapse, Air New Zealand posted the largest loss in the country's corporate history: $1.425 billion.

Over the first 10 years of the 21st century, however, a series of measures would see the carrier's balance sheet and reputation improve – as new routes, new aircraft and a commitment to service made it one of the world's top airlines.

Change was driven from the top but included the whole company. When Ralph Norris came on board as Chief Executive Officer in 2002, one of his first initiatives was a staff survey, which turned up worrying results – only 29 percent of staff even bothered to complete the survey. Of those, 90 percent said they had no confidence in management or the company's plans for the future. "And then," Norris told an interviewer, "the financial forecast identified there had been a $40 million negative movement in the profitability figures from the forecast year ending 2002."

What to do?

"Ralph focused on customer service," says a former colleague. "In those first couple of years we were dealing with an airline that got to 20 minutes away from bankruptcy and suffered because it was working with old equipment. But Ralph put people ahead of the equipment, and our staff did a fantastic job getting us through a tough period in the early days of rebuilding the airline."

Top Ralph Norris took over as CEO in 2002.

Right Rob Fyfe was appointed CEO in October 2005.

"If I have any real criticisms of the company when I joined it," Norris has said, "it would be a view that the business was all about flying planes – rather than about flying people."

A 30 percent pay cut for management and an end to perks such as chauffeur-driven cars helped restore staff confidence. "We went through a pretty significant reduction in the scale of the organisation," Norris told *iStart* magazine. "Forty percent of our management positions disappeared in the late part of 2001 and early 2002."

The staff were asked to take a pay pause. "A line was drawn under where we were," says a former member of the executive team. "We had to rebuild the airline and that was a very exciting time." It's not often you get an opportunity in a business to start again. Air New Zealand started changing its marketing and renegotiating agreements with travel companies. Norris brought in new blood, which included future CEO Rob Fyfe, and put together a strategising team called the Fifth Floor Project. Eighty people were given a blank piece of paper and asked to redesign the airline. The suggestions led to numerous debates and resulted in new plans that embraced change.

That included the internet, which gave it the ability to market without the costs of travel agents or TV advertising. Baggage handling was changed as charges were introduced, as were new fare structures and self-check-in kiosks. Within a short time, more than 50 percent of passengers were using this method – the highest take-up rate in the world. Some customers didn't like the reduced service, but many more did, and today these measures are standard.

It wasn't all about streamlining. Although the focus was on flying people not aircraft, the airline still had to have aircraft those people would want to fly in. That called for some brave decisions, including the move to replace the Boeing 747s with B777 wide-bodied jets. "Ralph made the big call about the 777s and replacing the domestic fleet with A320s," says Norm Thompson, former Deputy Chief Executive. "This was inspiring stuff. First you work on your people, then you give them great new assets to fly in."

The ageing fleet of B747s was upgraded, with the first refitted aircraft rolled out in 2005 and others following at the rate of one a month. And there was new product inside the aircraft: lie-flat seats in business class, the new premium economy class, and a new AVOD (audio-video-on-demand) system, which offered a raft of inflight entertainment including movies, TV shows, music and games, all delivered to passengers on their their own television screens.

"Lie-flat seats and premium economy took the whole airline to a new level of quality," says Thompson. "It was a big risk because the capital involved in new seats and video systems and planes is huge. But if we hadn't made those calls we would have been left behind."

As new aircraft and a fresh attitude came online, the airline introduced new destinations that underlined the country's focus on the Asia-Pacific region. In 2004, the airline introduced flights from Christchurch to Los Angeles, Wellington to Nadi and Christchurch to the Cook Islands; the next year it launched a weekly service to Niue, followed by Adelaide and Vanuatu in 2006 along with flights between Rotorua and Sydney. That same year, it introduced the only direct flights between Sydney and the Cook Islands. In 2007, it began flying the long haul over the Pacific to Vancouver.

But it was the airline's extension into Asia that really rang the changes. In April 2006, it launched its first flights to London via Hong Kong and by the end of the year it would be flying regular direct flights between Auckland and Shanghai; in 2008 it added Beijing – vital routes for Kiwis doing business in China.

The result? Ninety percent of international customers said they would recommend it to other travellers and by 2010, the airline had received multiple accolades – for its support of the arts and of sport, for being a company New Zealanders could trust, for representing this tiny country on the world stage. Air New Zealand was the most admired brand in the country.

With passenger numbers climbing rapidly on all its routes and the business in the black, the news was official: New Zealanders were back in love with their national airline.

Right The new-look airline included the hugely successful A320, which replaced the domestic fleet.

2000–2009

Switching gear

In 2005 the introduction of uniforms designed by leading New Zealand fashion house Zambesi marked the end of 18 months of collaboration between airline staff and the designers. The new wardrobe replaced the Barbara Lee uniform, which had done more than 20 years of service.

The new uniform featured a distinctly New Zealand colour palette mirroring the greenstone, teal, schist and slate hues of our land, sea and sky; a Maori motif created by the talented Derek Lardelli; soft fabric woven from the finest New Zealand merino wool; and hallmark curves inspired by the Koru.

The uniform was the final touch to the airline's new-look long-haul service, which was progressively introduced from August 2005. The new uniforms would be worn by cabin crew, pilots and airport staff. The management group were differentiated from general staff by the colour of their uniforms.

More than 5000 staff around the world stepped into the new Zambesi uniforms, six months after they were first revealed at Air New Zealand Fashion Week 2005.

Opposite Greenstone, teal, schist and slate made up the distinctly New Zealand colour palette.

Right The Zambesi uniform was the first change for staff in more than 20 years.

Below Inflight entertainment features the latest releases – in this case, *The Chronicles of Narnia: Prince Caspian*, from August 2008.

Above Children no longer rely simply on activity books to keep them occupied in flight.

Left An Air New Zealand aircraft with personal screens on every seat back.

Fun and games

Right, from top
Earlier incarnations of inflight entertainment: TEAL playing cards; pop-out stand-up models for junior Air New Zealand travellers; an NAC colouring book; a travel-themed colouring picture.

The opportunity to sit back and switch off is one of the biggest drawcards of flying, as compared to other forms of travel – but since the early days of commercial aviation, switching on has become an essential part of that experience.

Inflight entertainment has always been a crucial part of the flying experience. The earliest examples were a book or a pack of cards, but passenger flights hadn't been operating very long before the need to provide a diversion on long flights became apparent.

The first movie screened on a plane was a short film shown in 1921, but it wasn't until the wide availability of relatively compact 16mm film around 1960 that feature screenings became practical.

Early versions used a screen that was lowered at the front of each cabin and onto which a film was projected. Everyone watched the same movie at the same time. Well, almost. In the early days, the movie was relayed through the plane, so in theory, if you had a favourite bit, you could walk down the aisle and follow its progress to watch it again and again.

It's a sharp contrast to today, with hundreds of options screened to your personal entertainment centre, vastly improved sound systems, and flight mode allowing the use of personal devices becoming standard on flights.

Over the years, Air New Zealand flights have included performances by bands such as Opshop and Goodnight Nurse, but in general it's movies and television that help passengers pass the time.

As with every other aspect of flying, inflight entertainment is evolving, and fast. In the future passengers will be able to connect to the internet and use their own devices to watch content. And innovations such as Seatchat – effectively texting between passengers – and sophisticated inflight shopping options are soon to be introduced.

Although new-release movies are the most popular form of inflight entertainment, the humble audio component – which used to be all there was to complement the one movie screened – is adjusting to the post-digital age. "Where traditionally you plugged your headset into the seat arm and had 10 or 12 radio shows, with our new on-demand audio you can choose from 800 albums. The tone of hosted radio shows used to be cheesy but now we're working with radio networks to get a lot more energy into it," says an executive. Another looming innovation is multi-device use comparable to the common at-home scenario of being on the iPhone while watching TV.

For many passengers though, a pack of cards and a book are still their choice of inflight entertainment – the key is having the choice.

In the seat pocket in front of you

The magazine in the seat pocket in front of you is one of the earliest forms of inflight entertainment. A diverse mix of articles to help the flight pass more quickly, usually salted with some useful information about routes, aircraft features and safety matters, the inflight magazine is as much a part of the travel experience as seatbelts and overhead lockers.

The title of TEAL's inflight magazine *Flight Companion* describes perfectly this part of the magazines' function. Its other role was equally important – selling travel. Airlines are in the business of persuading people to leave home, and inspiring, entertaining stories about the airline's destinations are a big driver of business.

The current generation of magazines started with *Jetaway*, which was launched by Air New Zealand in 1966, followed by *Skyway*, *Pacific Way*, *Pacific Wave*, *Panorama*, *Air New Zealand* and, since 2007, *KiaOra*.

Air New Zealand's magazines have always been produced to a very high standard and have won numerous national and international awards, holding their own when competing against the best of around 150 inflight magazines produced worldwide.

Right TEAL's inflight magazine was a full-colour affair designed to inspire its passengers to travel to exotic locales both near and far.

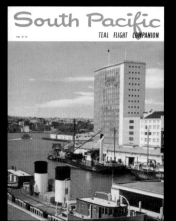

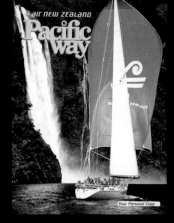

This page Air New Zealand's magazines have been through numerous incarnations since the 1970s but one thing has stayed the same: they've always been yours to take home.

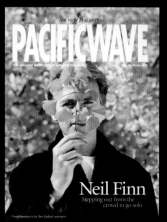

Above, from left From 2004, the magazine was called *Air New Zealand*, and in 2007 it was renamed *KiaOra*.

Coming back down to earth

Established in 2008, the Air New Zealand Environment Trust is an eco-conscious initiative designed to take action on the most urgent environmental issues, and to restore Aotearoa to its former glory. Traveller donations and company contributions have seen the programme go from strength to strength.

The trust's mission, as described on its website, is "to help restore our eco-systems, reconnect us with nature and make a positive difference in the world… take responsibility for some of the global and national environmental problems that upset the delicate balance of our planet. It will help communities, support projects, give grants, as well as fund research and development into ways to enhance New Zealand's environment. It is committed to regenerating or restoring our land to its original natural glory."

Former Air New Zealand Deputy Chief Executive Norm Thompson was chairman of the Trust and explains its workings.

"We set up the Environment Trust with seed money raised by giving customers the opportunity to donate through the internet when they made their bookings. For our part, the company used to and still does contribute a percentage of the business travel that we do. When anybody within the company travels internationally for business purposes, the emissions are calculated and we put more money into the trust to compensate for the emissions we have been responsible for.

"Our first project was growing a new forest at Mangarara Station in Hawke's Bay. We wanted the projects to have some sort of tourism benefit because that's the business we're in. So at Mangarara we planted more than 60,000 trees on land that was no good for anything. It will take time for that to grow into something substantial, but the people who own the land are in the throes of building a lodge and it will be turned into a tourism experience in the Hawke's Bay. The lodge sits in front of a beautiful lake, where there's wild duck and bird life, and behind the lodge is an escarpment that's been eroded over the years but is now being turned into a forest.

"We've got involved in another project on Motutapu Island in Auckland's Hauraki Gulf where revegetation is important. We invested in a nursery over there so the seedlings that have come from Motutapu have much stronger and quicker generation than where they were before.

"At Okarito on the West Coast we have what we call a cedar mountain experiment. A big escarpment there was being affected by farm run-off. We were losing kiwi and other bird life and natural ferns. So we got involved in replanting and clearing up the land. We embarked on a programme to eradicate pests such as rats, stoats and cats so the kiwi have a chance to breed and hatch. Now the lagoon looks stunning and we've seen kiwi return.

"On the Otago Peninsula, we've done a project with blue penguins. We were losing lots of eggs to pests, so we built an environmental fence around the area they come into, and we've built a platform where tourists can come and stand at night with a dull light and watch them coming in from the sea."

 Above One of the Environment Trust initiatives involves planting native trees on marginal hill country Mangarara Station in Hawke's Bay.

Right ANZET's partnership with the "Family Farm" at Mangarara began in 2008.

Far right Volunteers at the Trust's nursery on Motutapu Island in the Hauraki Gulf.

What a joke

Like all businesses, politicians, celebrities and individuals who find themselves in the public eye, Air New Zealand has been the butt of many a newspaper cartoonist's humour over the years.

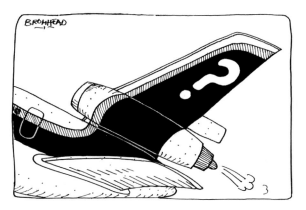

206 History: 2010–2015
Milestones and other
memorable moments
from the decade.

212 Trooping of the colour
Introduction of the new
Trelise Cooper-designed
uniforms.

214 Safe hands
From *The Bare Essentials*
to *Just Another Day in
Middle-earth*, Air New
Zealand's safety videos
never fail to captivate.

218 Chair leaders
The luxury seating
that revolutionised
long-haul travel.

220 Greener skies
Air New Zealand faces
climate change head-on.

224 Brought to you by
The high-profile
sponsorship taking the
best of New Zealand
to the world.

**230 Welcome to
Middle-earth**
How *The Hobbit* sent
New Zealand tourism
numbers soaring.

232 Black to the future
The first Boeing 787-9
Dreamliner is unveiled

234 From the flight deck
A message from
Air New Zealand CEO
Christopher Luxon.

236 Air New Zealand fleet
From the flying boats to
wide-bodied jets, and
everything in between
from 1940 to 2015.

2010–

=2015

The second decade of the 21st century saw the airline enter one of its most fertile and creative periods as it developed new ways of meeting customers' ever-changing needs. From the new uniforms designed by fashion doyenne Trelise Cooper to new livery, aircraft, fare structures, inflight entertainment options, safety videos and seats – everything was up for rethinking in the interests of creating a customer-focused business.

New technology was key here. As customers became more comfortable with digital commerce, the airline was able to offer more ways of using it, for instance by allowing them to choose a combination of seat and amenities when they booked online.

Among the most significant developments was the expansion of self check-in facilities to international flights. Air New Zealand also exported this technology to other countries such as Australia, where it had not been seen before.

And as its 75th anniversary year approached, in the most striking change to its livery in the company's history, the introduction of a black-and-white colour scheme was announced in 2012.

Every time a new plane is added to the fleet, excitement is generated within the airline and among the public, and these years saw the arrival of the first Boeing 777-300ER and the long-awaited Boeing 787-9.

Also this decade, the airline expanded its environmental focus with earth-friendly activities.

As well as improvements to the inflight experience there were innovations such as the OneSmart card which functioned as a debit card for overseas travellers but also tied with the Airpoints loyalty programme. Customer focus was repaid with increased customer loyalty and profits improved.

Air New Zealand had been an enthusiastic supporter of Peter Jackson's first *Lord of the Rings* trilogy, and with the release of *The Hobbit* series of three films, the airline ran a series of Hobbit-themed campaigns.

In 2011, when a series of earthquakes devastated the Canterbury region, Air New Zealand was there to help, moving more than 45,000 people out of Christchurch using every aircraft in its fleet. It also offered $50 fares for travellers, and assisted emergency services to get to the wrecked city in the days after the devastating quake.

As its 75th anniversary year approached, in the most striking change to its livery in the company's history, the introduction of a black-and-white colour scheme was announced in 2012.

Left Meals on longhaul flights have been devised by expert chefs including Peter Gordon.

Above and right Air New Zealand takes delivery of the world's first Boeing 787-9 Dreamliner painted in the company's new corporate livery.

8 January 2010
Trelise Cooper is announced as designer of Air New Zealand's next uniform.

January 2010
The Boeing 777-300's revolutionary interiors – including the economy Skycouch and premium economy Spaceseat – are unveiled.

February 2010
Air Transport World magazine names Air New Zealand Airline of the Year.

May 2010
Air New Zealand awarded Best Airline Australia/Pacific and the Staff Service Excellence Award for Australia/Pacific at the Skytrax Awards.

November 2010
UK consumer magazine *Which?* names Air New Zealand Best Airline for 2010.

Above 2010 saw the arrival of the new Trelise Cooper-designed uniform.

Below TV personality Bear Grylls starred in a new safety video which attracted global attention.

HISTORICAL EVENTS IN NEW ZEALAND
2010–2015

2010
- A magnitude 7.1 earthquake strikes the Canterbury region causing widespread damage to Christchurch and surrounding areas (left).
- An explosion in the Pike River mine (right) on the South Island West Coast kills 29 miners.

2011
- A magnitude 6.3 earthquake strikes Christchurch (left) causing widespread damage and 185 deaths.

1 June 2010

New self-check kiosks unveiled for trans-Tasman passengers. It is predicted that use of the kiosks will cut check-in times by half.

24 December 2010

Air New Zealand's first Boeing 777-300ER aircraft touches down in Auckland.

1 February 2011

The All Blacks A320 aircraft touches down at Auckland Airport – the A320 will eventually replace the 737-300 fleet.

7 February 2011

Air New Zealand, in partnership with Vodafone, announces new black A320 aircraft will have mobile phone and data capability.

22 February 2011

When a devastating 6.3 magnitude earthquake strikes the Canterbury region, 185 people are killed. In the following week Air New Zealand moves more than 45,000 passengers domestically out of Christchurch, using every aircraft in its fleet.

Top The B777-300ER resplendent in black livery.

Left Self check-in kiosks at Auckland Airport.

Right Air New Zealand played a big part in the early days after the 2012 Christchurch earthquake.

CHRISTCHURCH

- All Blacks win the Rugby World Cup against France, 8-7 at Eden Park, New Zealand (left).
- The container ship *Rena* runs aground on Astrolabe Reef, off Tauranga, resulting in New Zealand's worst oil spill (right).

2012

- New Zealand sends its biggest team to the London Olympic Games, and wins a total of 13 medals. Air New Zealand-sponsored canoeist Lisa Carrington (left) wins gold to clock up the nation's 100th Olympic medal.

- Marmageddon breaks out when it is announced that production of Marmite has been disrupted by the Canterbury earthquakes. The breakfast spread disappears from supermarket shelves.

- A tornado hits the suburb of Hobsonville in Auckland, causing widespread damage and killing three people.

12 May 2011
Skycouch wins the aviation category in *Condé Nast Traveller*'s 2011 Innovation and Design Awards.

23 June 2011
Air New Zealand collects three Skytrax World Airline Awards – Best Airline Australia/Pacific, World's Best Premium Economy Class Airline and World's Best Premium Economy Class Airline Catering.

22 November 2011
The OneSmart card, a prepaid MasterCard especially suitable for overseas travellers and that also offers Airpoints dollars, is launched. It promises to transform the traditional Airpoints card into the ultimate travel companion.

20 April 2012
Prime Minister John Key announces partnership between Air New Zealand and DOC, committing $4m worth of services to DOC to support biodiversity projects, endangered species transfers, and Great Walks marketing support.

13 July 2012
Air New Zealand announces a global three-movie partnership with *The Hobbit*, making it the official airline of Middle-earth.

18 September 2012
Air New Zealand announces it will contribute more than $1 million towards scientific research in Antarctica.

7 November 2012
Air New Zealand is the first airline to offer international customers the benefits of fast-track kiosk check-in facilities at Sydney Airport.
The first of Air New Zealand's much talked about Night Rider services takes off, with $29 fares between Auckland and Wellington.

Left Air New Zealand CEO Christopher Luxon.

Far left The Tongariro Crossing – one of the Department of Conservation's Great Walks, which Air New Zealand is proud to support.

2013
- Same-sex marriage is legalised (left).
- New Zealand loses its bid to win the America's Cup after a nail-biting series in San Francisco that captivated the nation.

- New Zealand's population reaches the 4.5 million mark, according to Statistics New Zealand estimates (right).

- The All Blacks win 14 tests in a row to become the first undefeated international rugby team in the professional era.

- Broadcaster and TV personality Sir Paul Holmes dies after a long battle with cancer.
- Production of Marmite resumes (right).

January 2013
Europe's Jet Airliner Crash Data Evaluation Centre names Air New Zealand one of the three safest airlines in the world.

January 2013
Christopher Luxon, formerly Group General Manager International Airline, takes over as Air New Zealand's new CEO.

21 March 2013
Air New Zealand is named New Zealand's most attractive employer for a third consecutive year at the Randstad Awards – the first time for an organisation anywhere in the world.

3 April 2013
Air New Zealand and Pratt and Whitney announce a joint investment of $20 million in new workshops and a logistics centre to support new generation aircraft at the jet engine overhaul facility at Christchurch Airport.

19 August 2013
A New Zealand same-sex couple ties the knot at 30,000ft to celebrate the legalisation of same-sex marriage.

24 September 2013
The first aircraft bearing the airline's New Zealand Fern Mark-inspired livery takes flight.

9 July 2014
Air New Zealand becomes the first airline in the world to take delivery of the Boeing 787-9.

23 July 2014
Air New Zealand announces that it will commemorate its 75th anniversary with an exhibition at the country's national museum, Te Papa in Wellington.

September 2014
Final Boeing 747 flight from San Francisco to Auckland.

Top right A couple was married at 30,000ft to celebrate the legalisation of same-sex marriage.

Right Air New Zealand takes delivery of the Boeing 787-9 Dreamliner.

2014
- Eleanor Catton's novel *The Luminaries* (right) wins the coveted Man Booker Prize for Fiction.

- Kiwi singer-songwriter Lorde (left) and producer and co-writer Joel Little win the Song of the Year Grammy for "Royals". Lorde also wins Best Pop Solo Performance.

- Royal heir Prince William visits New Zealand with his wife, the Duchess of Cambridge, and baby George (right).

- John Key's National Party wins a third term at the New Zealand elections after one of the most controversial campaigns in recent history.

Above The uniform for cabin crew is twilight pink to complement the new cabin interiors. Inflight managers are subtly highlighted with sky blue.

Trooping of the colour

In 2010 Air New Zealand announced that Trelise Cooper, another of New Zealand's leading fashion designers, had been engaged to design the next uniform. The mandate was that the uniform colour palette was to work in harmony with the newly unveiled aircraft interiors and reflect New Zealand themes with a cohesive visual uniformity while still allowing individual choice by addressing body type and personality preference.

For women, this included a variety of jacket, skirt and trouser options, as well as dresses, blouses and shirts. The collection has varying levels of formality, especially for cabin crew; one that provides a more formal look when travelling through airports and welcoming customers on board, changing to a more casual and friendly style once in the air.

Highlights of twilight pink for cabin crew, godzone green for ground staff and sky blue for ground and inflight managers are underpinned by black formal items such as suits and coats. Uniforms for inflight concierges, pilots and all other front-line work groups are included.

The change required a total of 90,000 garments to create a uniform that is now worn by more than 5000 staff.

Trelise Cooper's selection followed an extensive review of more than 25 New Zealand designers. She joined a prestigious line-up of designers who have lent their talent and skill to helping keep Air New Zealand as far ahead in the style stakes as it is among the world's airlines.

Left The uniform is underpinned by black formal items, including suits and coats.

Below A Kiwiana design livens up the back of an inflight manager's waistco

Safe hands

Air New Zealand's innovative and sometimes controversial safety videos have gone viral since day one, attracting more than 30 million online views, and counting.

To say that Air New Zealand has revolutionised the routine airline safety video in recent years is an understatement – or in the case of one of the first of them, an underwear statement.

The *Bare Essentials* safety video, which featured cabin and ground crew as well as then-Chief Executive Rob Fyfe demonstrating an aircraft's safety features in little more than liveried body paint, was first seen in 2009. It was tied to an advertising campaign promoting the message that Air New Zealand, unlike other airlines, did not have an array of hidden costs with which to surprise travellers.

"Within 10 days of hitting YouTube, the *Bare Essentials* inflight safety video had more than three million views," according to aviation writer Geoffrey Thomas, "and surpassed those for King of Pop Michael Jackson's final rehearsal footage. *Bare Essentials* became the number-one, most-viewed New Zealand travel video of all time on YouTube, surpassing the *Nothing to Hide* television commercial which sits at number two."

Air New Zealand's head of marketing Steve Bayliss said at the time that the airline had been "absolutely stunned" by the massive international interest. "In total, we've had around 6.5 million views on YouTube for the whole *Nothing to Hide* campaign, including views for our blooper and behind the scenes videos," he said. "By August 2010 the number of hits for both campaigns had soared past a staggering 11 million."

Realising they were on to a winner, the airline premiered a video the following year which gave All Blacks Richie McCaw, Mils Muliaina, Conrad Smith, Richard Kahui and then coach Graham Henry a chance to spread the safety word while displaying their comedy skills.

There followed videos featuring Rico the puppet, and Richard Simmons and Paul Henry, two polarising television personalities. The voices of TV stars Ed O'Neill and Melanie Lynskey featured in an animated video.

One of the most elaborate of the videos appeared in 2012 to tie with the airline's *The Hobbit* affiliations. It featured a cast of Hobbits, Dwarves, Orcs, and Sir Peter Jackson himself, and received more than 12 million views. The *Just Another Day in Middle-earth* video in 2013 further developed the Hobbit theme.

In partnership with DOC, British action television star Bear Grylls demonstrated safety procedures and showcased the New Zealand landscape in the *Bear Essentials of Safety* video, and for diehard TV addicts there was a chance to see *The Mary Tyler Moore Show*'s Betty White and Gavin MacLeod reunite as safety-conscious seniors in *Safety Old School Style*.

The safety videos have given the company a marketing edge even if, occasionally, they have been too edgy for some. That was certainly the case with the *Safety in Paradise* video, which celebrated 50 years of *Sports Illustrated* and the airline's commitment to the Cook Islands. It attracted controversy from the start and attracted more than 6.5 million YouTube views.

The innovative safety videos have been a cost-effective promotional bonanza for the airline, with more than 30 million online views and counting, and widespread coverage in major international print and broadcast media.

Left US fitness personality Richard Simmons put a leotard-clad cabin crew through their paces in the *Fit to Fly* safety video.

Below left The *Safety In Paradise* video polarised opinion but was a hit on YouTube.

Right UK television personality Bear Grylls careered around the Southern Alps in the *Bear Essentials of Safety* video.

Greener skies

The future of aviation may well depend on how positively it can respond to the challenges of climate change and ever-diminishing resources. Air New Zealand's range of environmental initiatives won it the Energy Efficiency and Conservation Authority's Supreme Award in 2012, and Best Global Tourism Business at the World Travel and Tourism Council's Tourism for Tomorrow Awards in 2013.

FUEL-EFFICIENT FLIGHT

Just a small deviation off course on a long-haul route can swallow up a huge amount of extra fuel. Accordingly, Air New Zealand has tried several innovative ways to keep its fuel consumption as low as possible. Lower fuel means lower costs which can turn into lower fares and increased profits, so this is truly a case where what is good for the planet is also good for business.

"As far as the company is concerned," says former Deputy CEO Norm Thompson, "we made a multi-million-dollar decision to try to get the most fuel-efficient aircraft. Chief Pilot David Morgan is very focused on making sure pilots are flying as efficiently as possible and not putting their feet down. We are flying as direct routes as we can to reduce fuel burn. His programmes have reduced pollution and saved us money on fuel.

"Meanwhile, on the ground our most recent project is the hangar at Auckland Airport where we've installed the largest set of solar panels in the country to generate power. Solar now makes a significant contribution to the electricity use at Auckland Tech Ops."

REQUIRED NAVIGATION PERFORMANCE

Air New Zealand flew its first RNP flight using a B737 on an Auckland to Queenstown flight in 2006.

RNP is a type of performance-based navigation that allows an aircraft to fly a specific path between two 3D-defined points in space. It includes a requirement for on-board navigation performance monitoring and alerting.

Simply put, the technology, which was fitted to the entire A320 fleet, allows pilots to fly at lower altitudes on a more precise and efficient route into an airport, saving fuel and emissions and reducing the impact of bad weather on services.

While the operational demands of landing in Queenstown drove Air New Zealand's push into RNP operations, another significant factor was the millions of tons of fuel and the consequent CO_2 emissions.

Because of its high-precision capability, RNP can save airlines millions of dollars in fuel costs by using much shorter – and mostly curved – approaches to airports.

It also enables Air New Zealand aircraft to carry heavier payloads out of airports surrounded with terrain and with obstacle-clearance problems. The RNP flight paths minimise the significance of these problems, reducing the occurrence of weight-imposed passenger or freight offloads.

BIOFUEL

A two-hour test flight on 30 December 2008, using a potentially miracle biofuel was hailed as a "significant milestone" in the development of sustainable environmental fuel, one of the holy grails of green flying. The experiment was a joint initiative between the airline, Boeing, Rolls-Royce and Honeywell's UOP.

The 2008 flight from Auckland Airport used a 50:50 blend of standard jet fuel and jatropha oil in one of the plane's four engines while testing engine and fuel-system performance in different operating conditions and at varying altitudes.

The jatropha biofuel performed well in a range of tests both on the ground and in the air. A weedy African bush that produces inedible oily seeds, the plant was sourced from environmentally sustainable farms in south-eastern Africa (Malawi, Mozambique and Tanzania) and India. It was selected because it is not a food crop and can be grown on land unsuitable for food production.

Subsequent problems with supply have hindered development of this biofuel: the world continues to look for alternatives.

Top right An alternative to fossil-based fuel is one of the holy grails of green flying.

Right *Jatropha curcas* is a tropical plant with high oil content.

Far right A worker shows the seeds of the jatropha plant at the Sun Biofuels company in Gondola, Manica Province, Mozambique.

2010–2015

ASPIRE

In September 2008, NZ8 to San Francisco was renamed *Aspire I*, and took part in a world-first test flight to demonstrate the potential for significantly reduced carbon emissions under optimal flight conditions. ASPIRE stands for Asia and South Pacific Initiative to Reduce Emissions, whose aim was to develop "one perfect flight".

Air New Zealand was the first airline to conduct an ASPIRE flight. The flight "exceeded all our expectations", according to Captain David Morgan. It used 4,600 litres, or four percent, less fuel than normal, using a host of strategies to minimise fuel use. This represented a saving of 12 tonnes of CO_2.

For the flight, Air New Zealand used "just in time refuelling" to finalise the fuel load once the actual passenger and cargo load was known.

Optimised taxi and departure procedures were provided by Air Traffic Control and satellite-based User Preferred Routes (UPR) with Dynamic Air Route Planning Systems (DARPS) were used to optimise cruise.

Approval was received for a tailored arrival – a continuous descent at idle thrust to land, which also keeps consumption down.

WINGLETS

Air New Zealand's Boeing 767s have blended winglets – wingtip extensions which reduce lift induced drag and provide some extra lift – which have saved 1.2 billion gallons of fuel and 11.5 million tonnes of CO_2 while reducing the aircrafts' noise footprint by 6.5 percent. In June 2013, the airline was the launch customer for the first of the new fuel-efficient Airbus A320s with "sharklet" wing-tip devices.

ZONAL DRYERS

Air New Zealand has committed to fitting its entire fleet with CTT Systems' Zonal Dryers. The electrically powered dryers reduce moisture trapped in insulation between the aircraft outer skin and cabin lining, lowering aircraft weight. The airline expects fleet-wide savings of 1.9 million litres of fuel annually owing to the dryers.

Below The Zonal Drying System – the leading method for preventing excess moisture in modern aircraft.

Bottom Air New Zealand estimates the winglets on a Boeing 767-300 will save more than six million litres of fuel and 16,000 tonnes of carbon emissions annually.

Below The phases of *Aspire I*'s "fuel optimised" flight from Auckland to San Francisco.

PHASE 1	PHASE 2	PHASE 3	PHASE 4	PHASE 5
Pre-flight, Taxi and Take Off	Departure and Climb	Enroute Cruise	Descent and Approach	Taxi and Arrival

Brought to you by

High-profile sponsorship activities covering all aspects of New Zealand life, from sport to the environment, have been a successful brand-marketing exercise for Air New Zealand, none more so than the partnership between the airline and Sir Peter Jackson's *The Lord of the Rings* and *The Hobbit* trilogies.

You can tell Air New Zealand's sponsorship activities are successful because most people could name at least one alignment the airline has, most likely those with the All Blacks and *The Lord of the Rings*.

But there are also important relationships with the likes of the Air New Zealand Wine Awards, for which the carrier has had naming rights over the nearly three decades the awards have existed – as well as Antarctica New Zealand and the Department of Conservation (DOC), notably its Great Walks.

Then there are brand ambassador relationships with individuals such as chef Peter Gordon, designer Trelise Cooper, or All Blacks captain Richie McCaw, and sponsorship of some of the nation's most successful Olympians including Hamish Carter, Valerie Adams and Mahe Drysdale.

"We're proud to work with and support a range of New Zealand's world-class people," says James Gibson, who has been closely involved with sponsorship activities over many years.

When deciding on a relationship, the principle the airline uses is "support for world-class New Zealand", he says. "We did some consumer research a couple of years ago, which indicated the public thought Air New Zealand should be about showcasing the best of New Zealand and taking it to the world, so that's what we do. We try to make sure there's a balance across social, cultural, environmental and economic development properties."

Not everything is as attention grabbing as an aircraft in *The Lord of the Rings* livery, yet the behind-the scenes work is just as important. The airline carries out vitally important species translocation for DOC, moving more than 1300 endangered animals since their contract with the department was formalised three years ago.

Such work can be high maintenance – moving kakapo from the deep south of the South Island to Little Barrier, for example, involves intense manual handling, and with fewer than 150 of the birds left, there's a a great deal riding on the success of the exercise.

But perhaps the one sponsorship to rule them all has been the incredibly successful partnership between the airline and Peter Jackson's *The Lord of the Rings* and *The Hobbit* trilogies.

Air New Zealand initially became known as the airline to Middle-earth back in 2002. This campaign was spearheaded by its 'Middle-earth Fleet' of four aircraft, which carried the message of New Zealand's starring role in the epic films into markets where destination New Zealand and the airline often struggled for awareness and share of marketing voice.

The relationship had dividends for all involved, the movie producers, the airline and, not least, New Zealand itself. The airline's programme of Hobbit-themed marketing campaigns in offshore markets boosted tourism to New Zealand – international visitor numbers have reached an all-time high and research shows *The Hobbit* is a major factor influencing people to holiday in New Zealand.

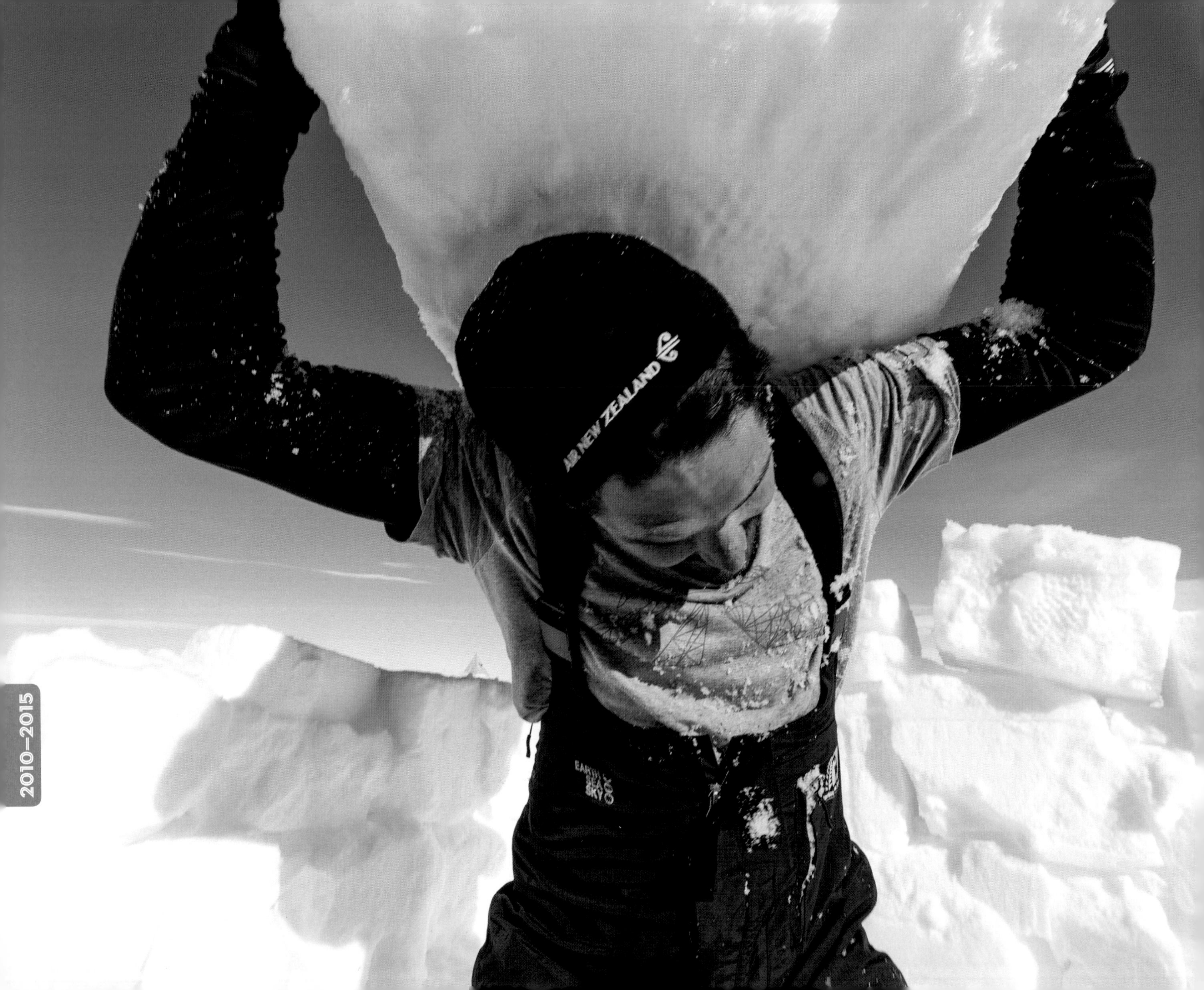
AIR NEW ZEALAND
EARTH SEA SKY

Left In late 2013, Air New Zealand launched their "no ordinary place, no ordinary assignment", a global search to find volunteers keen to share the wonders of the Antarctic frozen continent with the world.

Below Air New Zealand's partnership with DOC has successfully raised awareness of the nine Great Walks.

Right Air New Zealand has assisted DOC with several translocation projects as part of its sponsorship.

Below Air New Zealand has had naming rights to the annual wine awards for nearly three decades.

Right *Wanderer*, by Sue Cederman of Motueka, featured in a photoshoot in the new Boeing 777-300 premium economy cabin to promote the Brancott Estate World of WearableArt™.

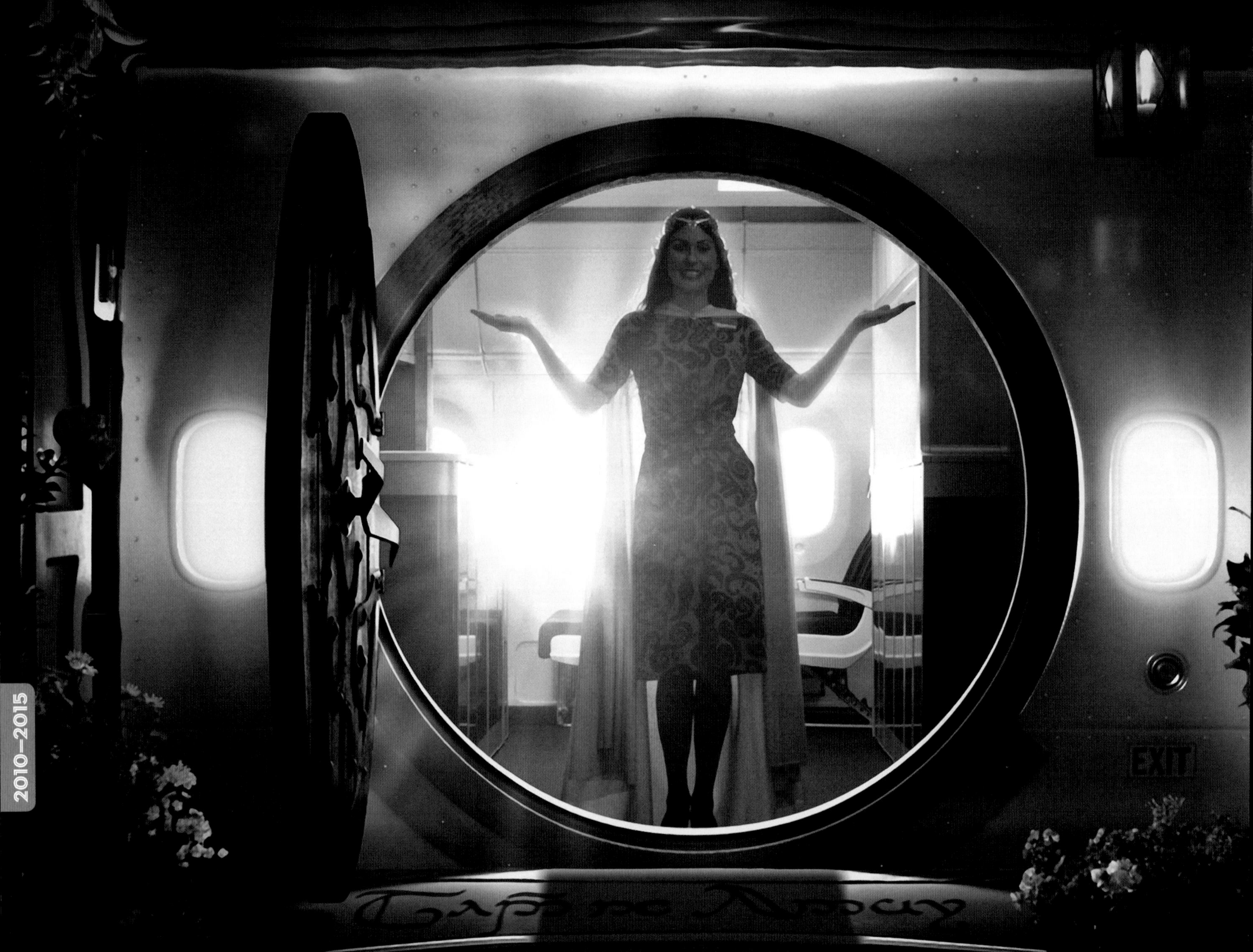
EXIT

Welcome to Middle-earth

A programme of Hobbit-themed campaigns in Air New Zealand's offshore markets boosted tourism to New Zealand considerably, with visitor numbers at an all-time high.

Left The safety video *Just Another Day in Middle-earth* captivated Tolkien fans around the world.

Below left Inflight magazine *KiaOra* ran special features on the launch of the trilogy.

Below The special Hobbit aircraft.

AIR NEW ZEALAND INFLIGHT MAGAZINE

KiaOra

2012

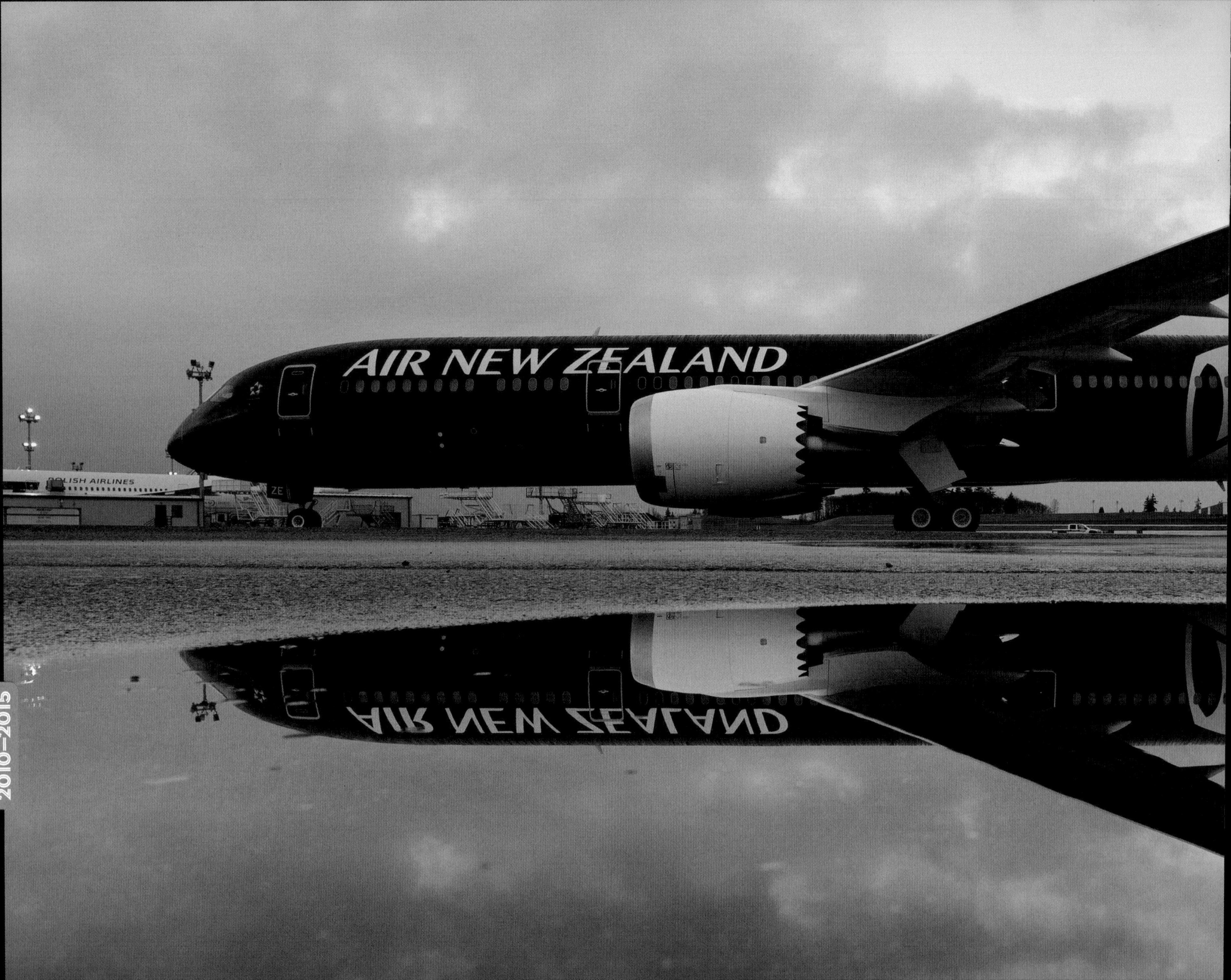
AIR NEW ZEALAND

Black to the future

At a much-anticipated ceremony in Seattle in April 2014, the aviation world got its first glimpse of the Boeing 787-9 Dreamliner, resplendent in Air New Zealand's classy new black-and-white livery, which incorporates the Air New Zealand Koru with Tourism New Zealand and New Zealand Trade and Enterprise's silver fern.

Left Air New Zealand's first Boeing 787-9 photographed at dawn after the first "reveal" at Boeing's Everett Field in Seattle.

From the flight deck

Air New Zealand is honoured to mark its 75th anniversary – a significant milestone and one that I believe all New Zealanders can be proud of.

As New Zealand's national carrier, Air New Zealand is an integral part of the history and fabric of the country and has played a crucial role in facilitating tourism, education, business and trade for more than seven decades.

I'm incredibly proud of what our airline has achieved – we've overcome some significant challenges throughout the years and emerged in an even stronger position than before. For this I must acknowledge those who came before me, and the Air New Zealanders all over the business who have worked tirelessly over the years to build the solid foundation and strong reputation that Air New Zealand continues to enjoy.

A lot has changed over the past 75 years – technology has certainly greatly enhanced the comfort and experience of flying. The one thing that has remained the same, however, is our airline's purpose to connect people, and always keep customers at the core of what we do. At the end of the day, we fly people not planes.

Looking to the future, I'm conscious that I won't be stewarding the airline forever, so my goal is to leave it stronger for future generations to lead and take forward.

To help us achieve this, we are significantly investing in further enhancing the customer experience through the purchase of new, state-of-the-art aircraft and the adoption of the very latest technologies to ensure travel on Air New Zealand is easy, seamless and, above all else, enjoyable.

We also continue to invest in our people. While many aspects of our business can be replicated, this is one area that cannot be copied and I truly believe our people are what sets us apart from our competitors.

So to all Air New Zealanders, past and present, to our customers, stakeholders, shareholders and friends – thank you for your continued support of Air New Zealand.

Here's to another 75 years.

Christopher Luxon
Air New Zealand CEO

Opposite Legendary pilot George Bolt at the controls of one of the early Solents.

Above Thanks to recent aircraft purchases, Air New Zealand is positioned well for the next 75 years. These images show the cockpit of the latest Boeings.

Air New Zealand Fleet 1940-2015

01. **Short S.30 Empire-class** (1940-47)
    🛈 19 ⏱ 257 kph

02. **Short S.25 Tasman-class Sandringham** (1946-50)
    🛈 30 ⏱ 274 kph

03. **Lockheed Electra 10A** (1947-50)
    🛈 10 ⏱ 298 kph

04. **Lockheed Lodestar** (1947-52)
    🛈 15 ⏱ 312 kph

05. **Short S.25 Sunderland Mk III** (1947-52)
    🛈 30 ⏱ 249 kph

06. **De Havilland DH83 Fox Moth** (1947-54)
    🛈 4 ⏱ 169 kph

07. **De Havilland Rapide & DH89B Dominie** (1947-64)
    🛈 5 ⏱ 211 kph

08. **Douglas DC-3** (1947-76)
    🛈 26 ⏱ 257 kph

09. **Short S.45 Solent Mk IV** (1949-60)
    🛈 45 ⏱ 322 kph
    Short S.45 Solent Mk III (1951-54)
    🛈 39 ⏱ 306 kph

10. **De Havilland DH114 Heron** (1952-57)
    🛈 14 ⏱ 266 kph

11. **Douglas DC-6** (1954-61)
    🛈 56 ⏱ 426 kph

12. **Vickers V807 Viscount** (1958-75)
    🛈 62 ⏱ 528 kph

13. **Lockheed L188C Electra** (1959-1972)
    🛈 71 ⏱ 644 kph

14. **Fokker F27-100 Friendship** (1960-90)
    🛈 40 ⏱ 435 kph

15. **Douglas DC-8 Series 52** (1965-89)
    🛈 155 ⏱ 860 kph

16. **Boeing 737-200** (1968-2005)
    🛈 98-117 ⏱ 788 kph

17. **Douglas DC 10 Series 30** (1973-86)
    🛈 268 ⏱ 880 kph

18. **Fokker F27-500 Friendship** (1973-90)
    🛈 48 ⏱ 450 kph

19. **Boeing 747-200** (1981-2000)
    🛈 385 ⏱ 905 kph

20. **Boeing 767-200** (1985-2005)
    🛈 209 ⏱ 850 kph

21. **Fairchild Metro III** (1988-2003)
    🛈 19 ⏱ 480 kph

22. **Boeing 747-400** (1989-2014)
    🛈 379 ⏱ 920 kph

23. **Saab 340A** (1990-2008)
    🛈 33 ⏱ 500kph

24. **Embraer EMB110-P1 (Bandeirante)** (1980-2002)
    🛈 15 ⏱ 341 kph

25. **Boeing 767-319ER** (1991-present)
    🛈 230 ⏱ 870 kph

26. **Boeing 737-300** (1998-present)
    🛈 133 ⏱ 790 kph

27. **ATR72-500** (1999-present)
    🛈 68 ⏱ 518 kph

28. **BAE 146-300** (2001-02)
    🛈 92 ⏱ 750 kph

29. **Beech 1900D** (2001-present)
    🛈 19 ⏱ 510 kph

30. **ATR72-200** (2004-05)
    🛈 66 ⏱ 518 kph

31. **A320-200** (2005-present)
    Short-haul
    🛈 168 ⏱ 850 kph
    Domestic
    🛈 171 ⏱ 850 kph

32. **Boeing 777-219ER** (2005-present)
    🛈 312 ⏱ 910 kph

33. **Bombardier Q300** (2005-present)
    🛈 50 ⏱ 520 kph

34. **Boeing 777-319ER** (2010-present)
    🛈 332 ⏱ 910 kph

35. **ATR72-600** (2012-present)
    🛈 68 ⏱ 518 kph

36. **Boeing 787-9** (2014-present)
    🛈 302 ⏱ 910 kph

🛈 = Maximum passengers
⏱ = Maximum cruising speed

Aircraft shown are not in exact proportion to each other.
Illustrations by Guy Body

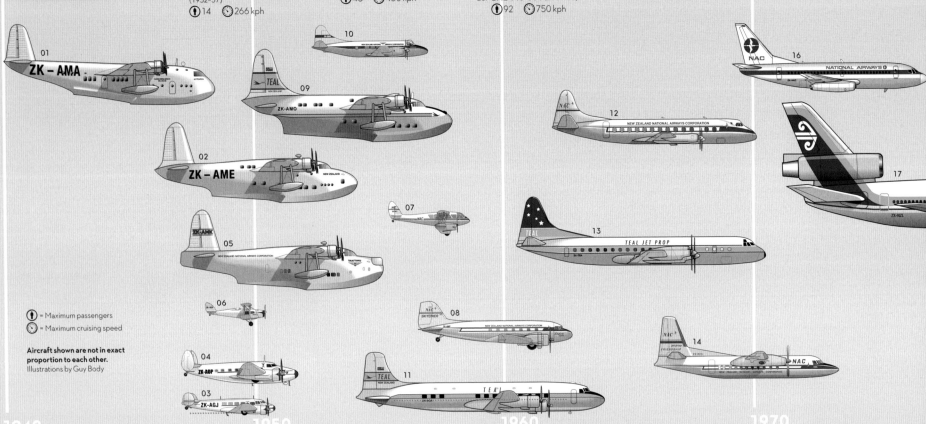

1940   1950   1960   1970

Illustrations

Pioneers

Page 6. Top row, from left: Science Photo Library via Getty Images; Mrs D, Thompson, postcard, Alexander Turnbull Library, PAColl-0892-12; Library of Congress, Prints & Photographs Division, photograph by Harris & Ewing, LC-DIG-hec-03507; Whites Aviation, (negatives, Alexander Turnbull Library), print courtesy Air New Zealand Ltd. Archive.

Middle row, from left: Anton Berntsen negatives relating the Walsh Brothers' Flying School, Alexander Turnbull Library, 1/4-123885-F; Sidney Clarence Gudsell Photographic Trust; WAC.2004.077.051.001. PRT, Walsh Memorial Library, The Museum of Transport and Technology (MOTAT); Arthur Ninnis Breckon, Alexander Turnbull Library, MNZ-2066-1/4-F.

Bottom row, from left: WAC.2004.077.061.001. PRT, Walsh Memorial Library, MOTAT; 75TH Anniversary Exhibition, 7111, Archives New Zealand, The Department of Internal Affairs Te Tari Taiwhenua; Alexander Turnbull Library, 1/2-015662-F; Photographer John King, Macmillan Brown Library, University of Canterbury.

7. *New Zealand Free Lance* photograph, Alexander Turnbull Library, 1/2-046051-F.

1940s

11. Clockwise from top right: Whites Aviation, Alexander Turnbull Library, Detail of WA-11687-G; WA-20530-G; WA-15850-F; WA-11274-G; WA-13383-F.

12. Main top to bottom: Whites Aviation, Alexander Turnbull Library, WA-07427-G; WA-11681-G.

Bottom left to right: Green & Hahn (Firm). Department of Internal Affairs, War History Branch, Alexander Turnbull Library, DA-07119-F; "Jockey" publicity photograph, Burt, Gordon H, 1924-1965, New Zealand, courtesy of Museum of New Zealand Te Papa Tongarewa, B.026680.

13. Main clockwise from top right: Whites Aviation, Alexander Turnbull Library, WA-06745-G, WA-04940-G; WA-04838-G. Air New Zealand Ltd. Archive, ANZ1011.3.

Bottom left to right: Photo by Keystone/Getty Images; Alexander Turnbull Library, 1/2-065969-F; PAColl-5567.

14–15. Left to right: Air New Zealand Ltd. Archive, 120A1741; Whites Aviation, Alexander Turnbull Library, WA-B2.

16. Whites Aviation, Alexander Turnbull Library, WA-24326-F.

17. Top: Air New Zealand Ltd. Archive, 2014.2.39.1.

Below left to right: Whites Aviation, Alexander Turnbull Library, Detail of WA-10945-G; WA-11149-G.

19. 2006/15:10:907:004, Wellington City Council Archives.

20. Left to right: Tasman Empire Airways Ltd.; C M Banks Ltd., Alexander Turnbull Library, Eph-D-AVIATION-1946-01; Tasman Empire Airways Ltd., Alexander Turnbull Library, Eph-E-AVIATION-TEAL-1950-01.

21. Top to bottom: Whites Aviation, Alexander Turnbull Library, WA-64898-F; WA-64899-F.

22–23. Whites Aviation, Alexander Turnbull Library, WA-03547-F; WA-05917-G.

24–25. Air New Zealand Ltd. Archive, 2014.3.51.4.

26. 2006/15:10:907:003 Wellington City Council Archives/Fairfax NZ.

27. Gordon Onslow Hilbury Burt, negatives, Alexander Turnbull Library, 1/2-037066-F.

28. Whites Aviation, Alexander Turnbull Library, WA-25876-G.

29. Clockwise from top left: *Evening Post* newspaper negative, Alexander Turnbull Library, 114/201/14-G; 2006/15:10:907, Wellington City Council Archives; *Evening Post* newspaper negative, Alexander Turnbull Library, 114/200/04-G.

30. Clockwise from top left: *Evening Post* newspaper negative, Alexander Turnbull Library, 114/309/13-G; Whites Aviation, Alexander Turnbull Library, WA-24054-F; WA-21856-F; WA-03073-G.

31. Whites Aviation, Alexander Turnbull Library, WA-01300-G.

32. NAC a report of progress, W & T Ltd., Alexander Turnbull Library, Eph-B-AVIATION-NAC-1952-01-front.

33. Top: New Zealand National Airways Corporation, Alexander Turnbull Library, Eph-E-AVIATION-NAC-1949-01.

Bottom: Air New Zealand Ltd. Archive, 2014.85.4.

34. Top: E V Paul, Government Printer, Alexander Turnbull Library, Eph-D-WAR-WII-1941-03.

Bottom: Air Force publicity brochure, Alexander Turnbull Library, Eph-D-WAR-WII-1941-04.

35. Whites Aviation, Alexander Turnbull Library, WA-03884-G.

36. Left to right: Whites Aviation, Alexander Turnbull Library, WA-20398-F; Air New Zealand Ltd. Archive, 2014.2.62.1.

37. Clockwise from left: Courtesy of the son of Bill Haythornthwaite; Arthur Alfred Thompson, Alexander Turnbull Library, Eph-E-AVIATION-TEAL-1950s-10; Poster, 'Fly to New Zealand', Arthur Thompson, early 1950s, New Zealand, courtesy of Museum of New Zealand Te Papa Tongarewa, GH009295; Arthur Alfred Thompson, Alexander Turnbull Library, Eph-E-AVIATION-TEAL-1950s-07; Eph-E-AVIATION-TEAL-1950s-02.

38. From top: Whites Aviation, Alexander Turnbull Library, WA-08117-F; WA-23003-F; Qantas Heritage Collection.

39. Clockwise from top left: Qantas Heritage Collection; Air New Zealand Ltd. Archive, 2014.258; Air New Zealand Ltd. Archive.

1950s

43. R. N. Smith Collection via AussieAirliners; Whites Aviation, Alexander Turnbull Library, WA-26907-F; F. Maurice Clarke Collection; Air New Zealand Ltd. Archive.

44. Main clockwise from top left: I & II, VC Browne & Son Aerial Photograph Collection; Image courtesy of Christchurch City Libraries, CCL-PhotoCD11-IMG0045; IV & V, VC Browne & Son Aerial Photograph Collection.

Bottom, left to right: Parliamentary portrait, Alexander Turnbull Library, 35mm-00094-D-F; Bert Snowden photograph, Alexander Turnbull Library, 1/2-029794-F.

45. Main clockwise from top left: F Maurice Clarke Collection; WA-31667-F; *Evening Post* newspaper negative, Alexander Turnbull Library, EP/1959/4368-F.

Bottom left to right: Ross White/ *The New Zealand Herald*; Photo courtesy of *Otago Daily Times*; Photo by Mondadori Portfolio via Getty Images/With permission of the Hillary Estate.

46. Main: *The New Zealand Herald*/Auckland War Memorial Museum PH-NEG-H958.

Bottom, left to right: *Evening Post* newspaper negative, Alexander Turnbull Library, EP/1955/2479-F; Photograph by Eric Lee-Johnson, 1956, courtesy of Museum of New Zealand Te Papa Tongarewa, O.030630; *New Zealand Free Lance* photograph, Alexander Turnbull Library, PAColl-5936-23.

47. Main clockwise from top right: Air New Zealand Ltd. Archive, 2013.1.121.01a; Whites Aviation, Alexander Turnbull Library, WA-45053P; Air New Zealand Ltd. Archive.

Bottom, left to right: Photo by John Claydon © Antarctica New Zealand Pictorial Collection TAE385 1957; *Evening Post* newspaper negative, Alexander Turnbull Library, EP/1958/2546-F; Photo by Central Press/ Hulton Archive/Getty Images.

48. Qantas Heritage Collection.

49. Top to bottom: Air New Zealand Ltd. Archive, 120A1754; Air New Zealand Ltd. Archive, menu; Tasman Empire Airways Limited Airline label, Alexander Turnbull Library, Eph-A-AVIATION-Labels-06.

50. Left to right: Air New Zealand Ltd. Archive, 120A1799; Detail of Tasman Empire Airways Limited pamphlet, Alexander Turnbull Library Eph-A-AVIATION-TEAL-1960-01; Walsh Memorial Library, MOTAT, WAC.2004.070.089.001.PRT; Air New Zealand Ltd. Archive, ANZ S1/10.

51. Left to right: Air New Zealand Ltd. Archive, 120A0229; Whites Aviation, Alexander Turnbull Library, WA-28878-G.

52. Left to right: Whites Aviation, Alexander Turnbull Library, WA-31531-F; Whites Aviation, Alexander Turnbull Library, WA-31664-F.

53. Whites Aviation, Alexander Turnbull Library, WA-31413-F.

54. Left to right: Tasman Empire Airways Ltd., Alexander Turnbull Library, Eph-E-AVIATION-TEAL-1950s-15/Son of Bill Haythornthwaite; Arthur Alfred Thompson, Alexander Turnbull Library, Eph-E-AVIATION-TEAL-1950s-06.

55. Left to right: Arthur Thompson poster courtesy of Museum of New Zealand Te Papa Tongarewa, GH009290; TEAL poster, Arthur Alfred Thompson, Alexander Turnbull Library, Eph-E-AVIATION-TEAL-1950s-05.

56. Image from justpacific.com

57. Top to bottom: Air New Zealand Ltd. Archive, October 81; Photo Courtesy of Peter Kilgour/Fairfax NZ.

58. Clockwise from top left: Air New Zealand Ltd. Archive; Air New Zealand Ltd. Archive, R103; 120A1989; Whites Aviation, Alexander Turnbull Library, WA-20544-F.

59. Images © Mirrorpix.

60. Clockwise from left: *Evening Post* newspaper negatives, Alexander Turnbull Library, EP/1959/3615-F, EP/1959/3616-F, EP/1959/3609-F.

61. Clockwise from top left: *Evening Post* newspaper negatives, Alexander Turnbull Library, EP/1959/3610-F; EP/1959/3613-F; EP/1959/3618-F; *New Zealand Free Lance* photograph, Alexander Turnbull Library, PAColl-8602-17; *Evening Post* newspaper negative, Alexander Turnbull Library, EP/1959/3520-F; *New Zealand Free Lance* photograph, Alexander Turnbull Library, PAColl-0785-1-026-14.

62. Air New Zealand Ltd. Archive, P113/With permission of the Hillary Estate.

63. Top to bottom: Auckland War Memorial Museum PH-CNEG-S508/With permission of the Hillary Estate; Air New Zealand Ltd. Archive, 2013.12.18/ With permission of the Hillary Estate; The New Zealand Herald/Auckland War Memorial Museum PH-NEG-H1821/With permission of the Hillary Estate; FPG/Getty Images/ With permission of the Hillary Estate.

64. Clockwise from left: Whites Aviation, Alexander Turnbull Library, WA-03093-F; WA-05899-G; WA-24166-F.

65. Left to right: Air New Zealand Ltd. Archive, s513, NAC ephemera, Archives New Zealand, The Department of Internal Affairs Te Tari Taiwhenua, AEPK 20231 W2774 Box 12, 001; AEPK 20231 W2774 Box 12, 006.

66. Clockwise from top left: Air New Zealand Ltd. Archive, I102; *Evening Post* newspaper negative, Alexander Turnbull Library, 114/349/12-F; Air New Zealand Ltd. Archive, 2014.1.13.58.1; Air New Zealand Ltd. Archive.

67. Clockwise from top left: George Bourne Collection, Auckland War Memorial Museum PH-NEG-C9615; *Evening Post* newspaper negative, Alexander Turnbull Library, 114/349/10-F; Associated Press of Great Britain Ltd. via F Maurice Clarke Collection; Whites Aviation, Alexander Turnbull Library, WA-25804-F.

1960s

71. Clockwise from top left: A Kemp/Fairfax Syndication; Air New Zealand Ltd. Archive, I139; Courtesy The Kauri Museum, Matakohe, NZ, Copyright Mervyn Sterling;

Air New Zealand Ltd. Archive, 2014.35.43.2; P135.

72. Main clockwise from top left: State Library of New South Wales 08763; 08765; Air New Zealand Ltd. Archive, A216.

Bottom left to right: Gordon Onslow Hilbury photograph, Alexander Turnbull Library, 1/2-036737-F; Reproduced with the permission of the estate of Barry Crump.

73. Main clockwise from top right: Staff Photographer for *The New Zealand Herald*; *The New Zealand Herald*; Matamata Historical Society, John Charles Collection; © Peter Lewis 2014.

Bottom left to right: Puke Ariki ARC2008-264; Guy Richardson Powles [Archives reference: AAQT 6401 A22,038], Archives New Zealand, The Department of Internal Affairs Te Tari Taiwhenua; Whanganui Regional Museum; Air New Zealand Ltd. Archive, 269.

74. Main top to bottom: Place setting, Crown Lynn Potteries Ltd., circa 1965, Auckland, courtesy of Museum of New Zealand Te Papa Tongarewa, GH012133/1-10; Gladys Mary Goodall, photograph, Alexander Turnbull Library GG-11-0760.

Bottom left to right: Sir George Grey Special Collections, Auckland Libraries; *The New Zealand Herald*.

75. Main left to right: Whites Aviation, Alexander Turnbull Library, WA-58754-G; Trevor Penman/Fairfax Media/ Auckland Libraries Footprints 02765 and courtesy of *Manukau Courier*; Charles Ulm National Aviation Collection/National Library of Australia.

Bottom left to right: Photograph by Revelle Jackson, Upper Hutt City Library Heritage Collections P1-1150-3540; Image

courtesy of Government House; *Evening Post* newspaper negative, Alexander Turnbull Library, EP/1968/1648a/1a-F.

76. A. Kemp/Fairfax Syndication.

77. Clockwise from top left: Morris James Hill, Negatives, Alexander Turnbull Library, 1/4-071858-F; 1/4-071859-F 35mm-18161-13-F; 1/4-071854-F.

78. Image courtesy of Wairarapa Archive.

79. Top to bottom: Air New Zealand Ltd. Archive, 2013.6.93.5; Air New Zealand Ltd. Archive.

80. Left to right: Air New Zealand Ltd. Archive, 120A2701; 2014.35.43.2; *Tealagram* Volume 4 no12.

81. Top row: S Lowe Collection; F Maurice Clarke Collection; S Lowe Collection.

Middle row: Air New Zealand Ltd. Archive, 2014.280.002a; Philatelic 'cover', 'First official direct air mail, Christchurch to Melbourne'; 29 June 1951, courtesy of Museum of New Zealand Te Papa Tongarewa, PH001085; F Maurice Clarke Collection.

Bottom row: Air New Zealand Ltd. Archive, R308988143; F Maurice Clarke Collection; Air New Zealand Ltd. Archive, 2013.4.26.1.

82. WAC.2008.117.2370.001. PRT, Walsh Memorial Library, MOTAT.

83. Top to bottom: WAC.2008.117.427.001. PRT, Walsh Memorial Library, MOTAT; Air New Zealand Ltd. Archive, K33111; Chris Lewis Photography.

84–85. All images courtesy of myvintagevogue.com

86. Left to right: Air New Zealand Ltd. Archive, I150; 2013.2.134.1.

87. All images Air New

Zealand Ltd. Archive: main, 2014.35.56.1; top, 2013.8.48.2; 2013.8.49.1, middle, 2013.8.6.2; 2013.8.23.1, bottom, 2013.6.42.1; 2013.5.

88. Clockwise from top left: Virtualworld image courtesy of Mark Cranston; Air New Zealand Archive, 2014.275.131; Air NZ Ltd. Archive.

89. Air New Zealand Ltd. Archive, 2013.2.81.1b.

90. Air New Zealand Ltd. Archive, 2014.15.35.

91. Left to right: Air New Zealand Ltd. Archive, *Air New Zealander* November 1965; 2014.15.9.

92. Air New Zealand Ltd. Archive, *Air New Zealander* November 1968.

93. NAC transparencies and prints, Archives New Zealand, The Department of Internal Affairs Te Tari Taiwhenua, AEPK 20231 W2774 Box 1; Air New Zealand Ltd. Archive, *Enzedair* May 1969.

94. Air New Zealand Ltd. Archive, Advert Hoardings February 1966.

95. Air New Zealand Ltd. Archive, I122.

96. Clockwise from top: I & II, Air New Zealand Ltd. Archive; Air New Zealand Ltd. Archive, Annual Report 1970–71.

97. Courtesy of F Maurice Clarke.

98. Courtesy of Dr Ross L Ewing.

99. Top to bottom: Photo courtesy of Raymond Massey; Whites Aviation, Alexander Turnbull Library, WA-65560-G.

100. Top: Air New Zealand Ltd. Archive, 120A1741; 2013.1.29.01.

Middle: Wellington City Council Archives AF077:8:4/01B; Air New Zealand Ltd. Archive, 2014.237.1; Wellington

City Council Archives, AF077:8:4/02; Air New Zealand Ltd. Archive, 2013.1.29.02.

Bottom: Wellington City Council Archives, AF077:8:4/02; Air New Zealand Ltd. Archive, 2014.2.48.2; Air New Zealand Ltd. Archive, 2013.1.29.03.

101. Top: Union Airways of New Zealand Ltd., Alexander Turnbull Library, Eph-A-AVIATION-1937-04; Air New Zealand Ltd. Archive; Air New Zealand Ltd. Archive, R308988148.

Middle: Air New Zealand Ltd. Archive, 2013.1.131.02b; 2014.41.74.1; 2014.41.74.1b.

Bottom: Air New Zealand Ltd. Archive, 2013.1.131.01; 2013.1.9.02b; Air New Zealand Ltd. Archive, R308988148.

1970s

105. Clockwise from top left: Air New Zealand Ltd. Archive, Annual Report 1985; Air New Zealand Ltd. Archive; Air New Zealand Archive; © Aviation History Collection/ Alamy; NAC transparencies, AEPK 20231 W2774 Box 12, Archives New Zealand, The Department of Internal Affairs Te Tari Taiwhenua,.

106. Main clockwise from top: Air New Zealand Ltd. Archive, Annual Report 1971–1972; Air New Zealand Ltd. Archive, 2014.178.31; 2013.6.16.1.

Bottom left to right: *Evening Post* newspaper negative, Alexander Turnbull Library, EP/1971/1880-F; Photo by Sylvia Pitcher/Redferns via Getty; Photo courtesy of *Otago Daily Times*.

107. Main top to bottom: Air New Zealand Ltd. Archive, 2014.267.003; © Bill Johnson/ Air New Zealand Ltd. Archive.

Bottom left to right: Council for Equal Pay and Opportunity, Alexander

Turnbull Library, Eph-A-WOMEN-1961-01; Badge, 'If it's safe', courtesy of Museum of New Zealand Te Papa Tongarewa, GH011827; New Zealand Post.

108. Main top to bottom: Air New Zealand Ltd. Archive, 2013.10.41.2; Royal Commission to Inquire into the crash on Mt Erebus [Archives Reference: ADQU 19628 COM49 40] Archives New Zealand, The Department of Internal Affairs Te Tari Taiwhenua.

Bottom left to right: *Evening Post* newspaper negative, Alexander Turnbull Library, EP/1975/0552X/23-F; New Zealand Maori Council Collection, Archives New Zealand, The Department of Internal Affairs Te Tari Taiwhenua, R21387570 AAMK W3495 Box 24/24t; Sandra Mu/Getty Images.

109. Main clockwise from top: Photo by Colin Monteath © Antarctica New Zealand Pictorial Collection ID1789 1979; Air New Zealand Archive, *Flying Times* September 1990; Fairfax NZ.

Bottom left to right: Colin McCahon, Partridge Street 1968, Photographer: Gordon H. Brown/Courtesy FHE Galleries; Mike Stephens/ Central Press/Hulton Archive/ Getty Images.

110. Whites Aviation, Alexander Turnbull Library, WA-26059-F.

111. K E Niven and Co. Commercial negatives, Alexander Turnbull Library, 1/2-226861-F.

112. Air New Zealand Ltd. Archive, I242.

113. Top to bottom: Air New Zealand Ltd. Archive; Air New Zealand Ltd. Archive, 2014.266.013.

114. Clockwise from top left: Air New Zealand Ltd. Archive, Annual Report 1984; 2014.267.015; 2014.267.016;

Annual Report 1986.

115. Top to bottom: Air New Zealand Ltd. Archive, Annual Report 1986; Annual Report 1976.

116–117. Left to right: Air New Zealand Ltd. Archive, 2013.1.157.01; 2013.1.205.01; 2013.1.225.01c; 2013.1.273.01.

118. Clockwise from left: Air New Zealand Ltd. Archive, 2013.1.125.01a; 2013.1.167.01; 2013.1.219.01c.

119. Clockwise from left: Air New Zealand Ltd. Archive, 2013.1.62.03a; 2013.1.89.02; 2013.1.267.01; NAC Coasters; 2013.1.103.01a.

120. Clockwise from left: Air New Zealand Ltd. Archive, 2013.1.117.01; 2013.1.81.01a; 2013.1.25.01b; 2013.1.69.01; NAC Coasters; 2013.1.145.01a; 2013.1.115.02a.

121. Air New Zealand Ltd. Archive, 2014.275.005.

122. *Evening Post* newspaper negative, Alexander Turnbull Library, EP/1957/3168-F.

123. Courtesy of Phillip Capper.

124. Clockwise from top left: Air New Zealand Ltd Archive, 2013.7.52.6; 2013.7.52.5; 2013.7.52.4; 2013.7.52.1; 2013.7.52.3; 2013.7.52.7.

125. Copyright Air New Zealand Ltd.

126. Air New Zealand Ltd. Archive, 2014.265.010.

127. Clockwise from top right: Air New Zealand Ltd. Archive/ Fairfax NZ; II & III, Air New Zealand Ltd Archive, *Jetaway* July 1976.

128. Top to bottom: Photo by Colin Monteath © Antarctica New Zealand Pictorial Collection ID6939 1979; Photo by Nigel Roberts © Antarctica New Zealand Pictorial Collection ID6936 1979.

129. Photo G. Lewis ©

Antarctica New Zealand Pictorial Collection 1979.

130. Photo Colin Monteath © Antarctica New Zealand Pictorial Collection 1979.

131. © Antarctica New Zealand Pictorial Collection 1979.

1980s

135. Clockwise from top left: Air New Zealand Ltd. Archive; Air New Zealand Ltd. Archive, K39550; Annual Report 1984; 2013.6.37.1a; 2013.6.37.3a; 2013.6.37.2a.

136. Main: *Report of the Royal Commission to inquire into the crash on Mt Erebus, Antarctica*, Crown Copyright.

Bottom left to right: Lisa Haun/ Contributor, Getty Images; *Evening Post* newspaper negative, Alexander Turnbull Library, EP/1981/2696/15.

137. Main clockwise top right: Air New Zealand Ltd. Archive; S. Lowe Collection; Air New Zealand Ltd. Archive, 2013.6.18.1b.

Bottom left to right: Stuart Menzies, *Evening Post* and *Dominion* newspapers, Alexander Turnbull Library, fl 1981–2004; Courtesy of St. Margaret's College and Christchurch City Libraries; *Evening Post* and *Dominion* newspapers, Alexander Turnbull Library, EP-Royalty-Charles, Diana and William-1983 tour-01; Alan Stevenson, *Evening Post* newspaper negative, Alexander Turnbull Library, EP/1977/3688/4-F.

138. Main top to bottom: ©Vaticano/Air New Zealand Ltd. Archive, 2014.51.6, Image courtesy of Jill Gardner; Image courtesy of Colin Zuppicich.

Bottom left to right: Ross White/AFP/Getty Images; Phil Reid, *Evening Post* newspaper negative, Alexander Turnbull Library, EP/1985/1233/11.

139. Main top to bottom: Copyright Air New Zealand Ltd.; II & III, S. Lowe Collection.

Bottom left to right: Bob Thomas/Getty; *Evening Post* newspaper negative, Alexander Turnbull Library, EP/1987/2998/22-F; South Canterbury Museum, L2012/007-027.

140–141. Air New Zealand Ltd. Archive, K39491.

142. Left to right: Air New Zealand Ltd. Archive, 2013.8.38.1; 2013.8.38.2.

143. Air New Zealand Ltd. Archive, Annual Report 1983.

144. Left to right: I & II, Air New Zealand Ltd. Archive, *Flying Times* March 1987.

145. Air New Zealand Ltd. Archive, Annual Report 1987.

146. Air New Zealand Ltd. Archive, 2013.6.37.5a.

147. Clockwise from left: Air New Zealand Ltd. Archive, 2013.5.61.1; 2014.99.102.10; 2013.6.111.3b; 2013.6.111.8.

148. Left to right: I & II, Air New Zealand Ltd. Archive, 2013.6.111.1a; 2013.7.74.1.

149. Air New Zealand Ltd. Archive, 2013.5.15.1.

150. Top to bottom: Air New Zealand Ltd. Archive; Copyright Air New Zealand Ltd.

151. Clockwise from top left: I & II, Copyright Air New Zealand Ltd.; III & IV, Courtesy of Phillip Capper.

152. Geoff Dale for *The New Zealand Herald*.

153. Clockwise from top: Air New Zealand Ltd. Archive; Courtesy of Dave Paull; S. Lowe Collection.

154. Merv Griffiths negatives of the *Evening Post* newspaper, Alexander Turnbull Library, EP/1985/4070/32-F.

155. *Air New Zealand News*,

October 11, 1979.

156–157. Nick Servian/ photonewzealand.

1990s

161. Clockwise from left: Air New Zealand Ltd. Archive, uniform number 265; © Blaine Harrington III/Alamy; New Zealand Post; *Evening Post* newspaper negative, Alexander Turnbull Library, EP/1987/2949/25A-F.

162. Main left to right: Air New Zealand Archive, Annual Report 1988; Air New Zealand Ltd. Archive.

Bottom left to right: Courtesy of Government House; Reserve Bank of New Zealand; Photo courtesy of *Otago Daily Times*.

163. Main: Ross Land/Getty Images.

Bottom left to right: Lloyd Homer, GNS Science; Anthony Phelps/Photosport; Photosport.

164. Main left to right: Reuters; Vince Bucci/AFP/ Getty Images.

Bottom left to right: Tim Clary/AFP/Getty Images; Marilynn Young/AFP/Getty Images; Photograph taken by Craig Simcox. *Evening Post* newspaper negatives, Alexander Turnbull Library, EP/1995/4228a/1a-F.

165. Main: Image courtesy of aero_icarus on flickr, CC.

Bottom left to right: Photograph by Ross Giblin. Dominion Post Collection (PAColl-7327), Alexander Turnbull Library, EP-1996-3628B; Barry Durrant/Getty Images; Photo by Ross Land/ Getty Images.

166. Top to bottom: Air New Zealand Ltd. Archive, Annual Report 1990; Air New Zealand Ltd. Archive, *Flying Times* June 1990.

167. Copyright Air New Zealand Ltd

168. Whites Aviation, Alexander Turnbull Library, WA-02990-F.

169. Top to bottom: Whites Aviation, Alexander Turnbull Library, WA-11167-G; WA-22618-F; Air New Zealand Ltd. Archive.

170. Whites Aviation, Alexander Turnbull Library, WA-10977-G, WA-02991-F. WA-22617-F.

171. Air New Zealand Ltd. Archive.

172. Air New Zealand Ltd. Archive, Annual Report 1993.

173. Air New Zealand Ltd. Archive, Annual Report 1992.

174. Clockwise from left: Air New Zealand Ltd. Archive, 120A5312; Air New Zealand Ltd. Archive; Air New Zealand Ltd. Archive, 2014.99.66.2.

175. Left to right: Sparrow Industrial Pictures Ltd./Air New Zealand Ltd. Archive, 2014.266.028a; Air New Zealand Ltd. Archive, 2013.5.25.4.2a.

176. Top to bottom: WPC.2002.1417.001.PRT, Walsh Memorial Library, MOTAT; Air New Zealand Ltd. Archive, 3-344; Virtualworld image courtesy of Mark Cranston.

177. Clockwise from top left: Air New Zealand Ltd. Archive, 2014.264; Air New Zealand Ltd. Archive, 2014.264; Chris Lewis Photography Ltd.

179. *Evening Post* newspaper negative, Alexander Turnbull Library, EP/1999/2753/17.

180. Loui Seselja. National Library of Australia.

181. Top to bottom: Geoff Pryor, National Library of Australia; Alan Moir, National Library of Australia; Al Nisbet, Fairfax NZ.

2000s

185. Clockwise from left: Copyright Air New Zealand Ltd.

186. Bottom: Photo by Joe Traver/Liaison Agency/Getty Images.

187. Main top to bottom: Courtesy of Pratt and Whitney Christchurch Engine Centre; Copyright Air New Zealand Ltd.

Bottom left to right: First civil union at the inner-Auckland Anglican church of St Matthews in the City in 2005, part of the regular Auckland Rainbow Community Church service, Karen Masters; Dean Purcell for *The New Zealand Herald*.

188. Main top to bottom: Photo courtesy of Mark Price/ *Otago Daily Times*; Copyright Air New Zealand Ltd.

Bottom left to right: Copyright Air New Zealand Ltd.; Photo by Mark Mitchell for *The New Zealand Herald*.

189. Top to bottom: AFP/ Getty; Copyright Air New Zealand Ltd.

Bottom left to right: Jamie Squire/Getty Images; Brendon O'Hagan/AFP/Getty Images, With permission of the Hillary Estate; Image courtesy of the United Nations Development Programme.

190. Copyright Air New Zealand Ltd.

191. Top to bottom: Dean Purcell/Getty Images; Brett Phibbs/*The New Zealand Herald*.

192–193. John Stewart LPSNZ.

194–195. Copyright Air New Zealand Ltd.

196. Clockwise from top left: *KiaOra* August 2008, Courtesy of Bauer Media Group; II & III, Copyright Air New Zealand Ltd.

197. Top to bottom: Air New Zealand Ltd. Archive, 120A1788; 2014.41.15.1; 2013.1.59.02a; 2013.1.59.02b.

198. Clockwise from top: South Pacific TEAL Flight

Companion periodical, Alexander Turnbull Library; Air New Zealand Ltd. Archive; South Pacific TEAL Flight Companion periodical, Alexander Turnbull Library.

199. Clockwise from top left: Air New Zealand Ltd. Archive, *Air New Zealand* May 1978; Air New Zealand serials, Alexander Turnbull Library, *Jetaway* December/ February 1979/1980; *Pacific Way* January/February 1986; *Pacific Way* May 1988; *Air New Zealand* November 2002 inflight magazine; *KiaOra* October 2012, Courtesy of Bauer Media Group; *KiaOra* September 2014, Courtesy of Bauer Media Group; Air New Zealand serials, Alexander Turnbull Library, *Pacific Wave* July 1998; *Pacific Wave* April 1999; *Skyway* December 1983; Air New Zealand Ltd. Archive, *Air New Zealand* June 1978; *Skyway* June 1980; Air New Zealand serials, Alexander Turnbull Library, *Jetaway* May/June 1983; *Panorama* March 2001; *Air New Zealand* January 2007; *Air New Zealand* September 2005.Copyright Air New Zealand Ltd.

200. Top to bottom: Images courtesy of Blue Penguins Pukekura.

201. Clockwise from left: Warren Buckland for *The Hawke's Bay Today*/Newspix; Image courtesy of Air New Zealand Environmental Trust; Image courtesy of Greg Hart.

202. Top left to right: Paul Ekers, *The New Zealand Herald*, Alexander Turnbull Library, DCDL-0026451; Paul Ekers, Alexander Turnbull Library, DX-017-004.

Middle left to right: Thomas Scott, *Dominion Post*, Alexander Turnbull Library, DCDL-0017050; Malcolm Paul Evans, *The New Zealand Herald*, Alexander Turnbull Library, DX-002-057.

Bottom left to right: Les Gibbard/ *The New Zealand*

Herald; Rod Emerson/ *The New Zealand Herald*/ Newspix.

203. Top left to right: © Neville Lodge/Air New Zealand Ltd. Archive, 2014.22.1; Laurence Clark, 'Klarc', *The New Zealand Herald*, Alexander Turnbull Library, H-171-001; Allan Charles Hawkey, *Waikato Times*, Alexander Turnbull Library, DX-014-022.

Middle left to right: © Neil Lonsdale/Air New Zealand Ltd Archive, 2014.22.3; Allan Charles Hawkey, *Waikato Times*, Alexander Turnbull Library, DCDL-0004374; Ekers, Paul, *The New Zealand Herald*, Alexander Turnbull Library, DCDL-0002385.

Bottom left to right: Peter Bromhead, *Auckland Star*, Alexander Turnbull Library A-333-046; Malcolm Walker, *Sunday News*, Alexander Turnbull Library, DCDL-0009285; Mark Winter, *Southland Times*, Alexander Turnbull Library, DCDL-0013473.

2010s

207. Copyright © Boeing; further images Copyright Air New Zealand Ltd.

208. Main top to bottom: Images Copyright Air New Zealand Ltd.

Bottom left to right: *The Press*/Fairfax NZ; Mark Mitchell/*The New Zealand Herald*/*The Press*/Fairfax NZ.

209. Main clockwise from top left: All Copyright Air New Zealand Ltd.

Bottom left to right: Paul Estcourt/ *The New Zealand Herald*; Christine Cornege/ *The New Zealand Herald*; Attila Kisbenedek/AFP/Getty Images.

210. Main left to right: Image is the property of Jimmy Johnson, Department of Conservation.

Bottom left to right: Hagen Hopkins/Getty Images;

Abaconda Management Group on flickr Creative Commons.

211. Main top to bottom: Copyright Air New Zealand, Ltd. Brett Phibbs/*The New Zealand Herald*.

Bottom left to right: Sanitarium New Zealand; Victoria University Press; Francis Specker/CBS via Getty Image; Mark Mitchel/*The New Zealand Herald*.

212–221. Copyright Air New Zealand Ltd.

222. Clockwise from top: Mike Millett/NZPA/Fairfax NZ; Carlos Litulo/AFP/Getty Images; Universal Images Group via Getty Images.

223. Clockwise from top right: Courtesy of CTT Systems AB; Fairfax NZ; Copyright Air New Zealand Ltd.

225–230. Copyright Air New Zealand Ltd.

231. Left to right: *KiaOra* December 2012, Courtesy of Bauer Media Group; Copyright Air New Zealand Ltd

232–233. Brett Phibbs/*The New Zealand Herald*.

234. Whites Aviation, Alexander Turnbull Library, WA-10592-G.

235. Top to bottom: © David Eyre; Nick Servian/ photonewzealand.

We have made reasonable inquiries to try and identify who owns the copyright of the images that appear in this publication. If you think you are the owner of any rights in any images, please contact us at Brand Manager, Air New Zealand, Private Bag 92007, Auckland 1010, and we will endeavour to reach a suitable arrangement with you.

Air New Zealand's first
Boeing 787-9 Dreamliner
on the tarmac at Everett
Field in Seattle.

Thanks and Acknowledgements

Among the most important books consulted for this publication were:

— *Conquering Isolation: The First 50 Years of Air New Zealand* by Neil Rennie, Heineman Reed, 1990

— *The Air New Zealand Story* by Geoffrey Thomas, unpublished MS

— *A History Of Teal: The Origins of Air New Zealand as an International Airline 1940–1967*, unpublished thesis by I. A. Thomson, 1968

— *The Way It Used to Be: A Back Room Anthology* by James Martin, unpublished

— An article by Michael Smythe in *ProDesign* magazine was an invaluable source of information on the origins of Teal, NAC and Air New Zealand livery.

Grateful thanks for their time and memories must be given to Dorothy McGillivray, Janet Beech, Kevin and Adrienne Berry, Nobby Clark, Ian Coburn, Henry De Silva, Richard Gates, Maynard Hawkins, Roger Poulton, Norm Thompson and Richard Williams. And all the other Air New Zealanders, past and present, who have contributed.

This book would not have been possible without the research assistance at Air New Zealand from Andrea Dale, Andrea Hemmins and Christine Whittle.